Cyber Bullying

Featuring Texter and Internetta

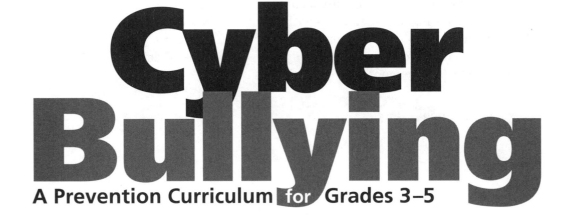

Cyber Bullying

A Prevention Curriculum for Grades 3–5

Susan P. Limber, Ph.D.

Robin M. Kowalski, Ph.D.

Patricia W. Agatston, Ph.D.

HAZELDEN®

ENDOWING LEADERSHIP AND LEARNING

Hazelden
Center City, Minnesota 55012
hazelden.org

ISBN: 978-1-59285-715-9

12   11   4   5   6

Cover design by Kinne Design
Interior design and typesetting by Kinne Design
Illustrations by Chris Dyrud

"Research indicates that incidents of cyber bullying begin when young people more actively use communication technologies—starting around third grade. This new curriculum is perfectly designed to help elementary students get started in the online world in a manner that will promote civility, rather than cruelty."

— Nancy Willard, M.S., J.D., author of *Cyberbullying and Cyberthreats: Responding to the Challenge of Online Social Aggression, Threats, and Distress* and executive director of the Center for Safe and Responsible Internet Use

"Helping parents and educators understand and address cyber bullying is the need of the hour. This practical curriculum has everything schools—not just teachers—need to develop not only a solid anti–cyber bullying program but also a foundation for digital citizenship training. There are also great ideas for parents and everyone who works with kids to teach and model empathy—what we all need to defeat all forms of aggression."

— Anne Collier, codirector of ConnectSafely.org, and founder and CEO of Tech Parenting Group

Contents

Duplicating this page is illegal. Do not copy this material without written permission from the publisher.

vii

Acknowledgments

We are indebted to Minerva Baumann, Marcy V. Azcarate, and Erika Orona for their insightful feedback on an earlier draft of this curriculum. We thank Hazelden's talented editorial team of Bonnie Dudovitz, Pamela Foster, and Sue Thomas for their tremendous assistance with this project—from its conceptualization to its final editing. Finally, we thank our wonderful families—Andrew, Austin, Jack, Noah, Jordan, and Mary—who inspire and support us.

How to Access the Resources on the CD-ROM

The accompanying CD-ROM contains print resources, including electronic versions of the curriculum's handouts and templates and related research information. All of these resources are in PDF format and can be accessed using Adobe Reader.® If you do not have Adobe Reader,® you can download it for free at www.adobe.com.

Whenever you see this icon ⬚ in this guide, this means the needed resource is located on the CD-ROM. The notation that follows this icon indicates the document number for that resource's file. The first letter or letter/number pair indicates which folder the file is located in on the CD-ROM. The CD-ROM file numbers will help you easily locate and print the resource you are looking for. This symbol (SP) indicates the document is also available in Spanish.

To access these print resources, put the disk in your computer's CD-ROM player. Open your version of Adobe Reader.® Then open the documents by finding them on your CD-ROM drive. These resources cannot be modified, but they may be printed for use without concern for copyright infringement. For a list of what is contained on the CD-ROM, see the Read Me First document on the CD-ROM.

Duplicating this page is illegal. Do not copy this material without written permission from the publisher.

xi

Introductory Materials

Introduction to the Curriculum

What Is *Cyber Bullying: A Prevention Curriculum for Grades 3–5?*

Cyber Bullying: A Prevention Curriculum for Grades 3–5 is a program that deals with attitudes and behaviors associated with cyber bullying. It consists of a five-session curriculum with additional resources on a CD-ROM including

- reproducible parent/guardian resources
- program posters and all student handouts
- resources to address cyber bullying schoolwide (establishing a school policy, addressing legal concerns, etc.)
- a short training on cyber bullying for program facilitators
- an optional pre-test/post-test that can be conducted before and after implementation of the curriculum to measure student retention

Most materials needed to implement the program are included in this manual and CD-ROM. In addition, a Web site has been established that will provide up-to-date information about cyber bullying. This Web site can be accessed at www.hazelden.org/cyberbullying.

What Are the Goals of the Program?

This program strives to

- raise students' and parents' awareness of what cyber bullying is and why it is so harmful
- equip students with the skills and resources to treat each other respectfully when using cyber technologies
- give students information about how to get help if they or others they know are being cyber bullied
- teach students how to use cyber technologies in positive ways

For more information on the learner outcomes for each session, turn to the curriculum's Scope and Sequence on pages 17–18.

What Are the Components of *Cyber Bullying: A Prevention Curriculum for Grades 3–5?*

Five-Session Curriculum

This curriculum consists of five 40-minute classroom sessions to be taught weekly. Each session includes Student Learner Outcomes and Parent/Guardian Learner Outcomes. Each session begins with a story about two upper-elementary school students, Texter (he is a text messaging expert) and Internetta (she is Internet savvy). The two characters serve as role models as they share their experiences with helping their friends deal with cyber issues, including cyber bullying. After each session's story has been read aloud, the teacher will lead the students in a large-group discussion, which may include a transparency or LCD projection or a poster. The second part of each session is an activity or game that integrates the content of the story and discussion. You may wish to provide extra time for students to work on some of these activities.

It is highly recommended that educators implement this program as part of an ongoing, comprehensive bullying prevention effort, such as the *Olweus Bullying Prevention Program (OBPP)*. More information on linking this curriculum to *OBPP* is provided on the CD-ROM. The Scope and Sequence for the five sessions is provided on pages 17–18.

You will also find a Glossary of Cyber Terms on pages 33–36 and on the CD-ROM for your reference and for you to send home to parents and guardians.

Parent/Guardian Materials

As with every strong prevention effort, it's important to actively involve your students' parents or guardians when implementing this program. Pages 29–31 presents a parent/guardian letter that informs parents and guardians about *Cyber Bullying: A Prevention Curriculum for Grades 3–5*. (This letter is also located on the CD-ROM.) It is recommended that this letter be sent out to parents or guardians prior to implementing the program, along with the Glossary of Cyber Terms on pages 33–36 and Internet Safety Tips for Parents and Guardians on pages 37–40. (These documents can also be printed from the CD-ROM.)

Each session includes a homework assignment to be done with a parent or guardian. (This will help achieve the Parent/Guardian Learner Outcomes.)

If a parent or guardian is unable to do the assignment with the student, then another close adult, such as a relative, neighbor, or caregiver, can complete it with him or her. The homework includes important information for parents and guardians about cyber bullying and Internet safety. There are two activities for students and adults to do together, including making family Internet safety rules and knowing what to do if cyber bullying occurs. Each homework assignment includes a return slip for parents/guardians and students to fill out and sign. Students will bring the return slip back to school so that the teacher will know the homework was completed.

All parent/guardian materials are provided in both English and Spanish.

Teacher Training Outline

You may want to multiply your efforts by training others to use *Cyber Bullying.* An outline for a three-hour training is provided on pages 97–102. Consider hosting a training session for your school's faculty.

Teacher Training Presentation

Included on the CD-ROM is a training presentation that includes in-depth information and statistics on cyber bullying. This training can be used as either a self-led training or as part of the Teacher Training Outline. Instructions on how to access and use this training are included on the CD-ROM.

I-13

Who Is the Intended Audience?

Cyber Bullying: A Prevention Curriculum for Grades 3–5 is designed for upper-elementary school students. This program would fit well within a health education, communications, technology, or general life skills curriculum (see references to national academic standards on pages 19–20). Teachers may use their discretion to adapt some activities to the age and maturity level of their students.

As noted earlier, the curriculum is most effectively used as part of a broad, ongoing bullying prevention program, such as Hazelden's *Olweus Bullying Prevention Program,* or as part of a general violence prevention effort.

A school counselor could offer *Cyber Bullying* as part of a support group or counseling or education program, or it could be used in after-school, community, youth enrichment (such as YMCA or Scouts), and faith-based youth programs.

Is This a Research-Based Program?

Cyber Bullying is not a research-based program, but it is based on the latest research in prevention and the topic of cyber bullying. Many of the lesson activities are patterned after prevention models that research has shown to be effective in decreasing negative student behavior and increasing student attitudes toward refraining from negative behaviors.

These strategies include providing parent-student activities, doing cooperative learning activities, and identifying why students behave as they do.

The curriculum also recommends that schoolwide policies and procedures be established that can effectively address the issue of cyber bullying in a broad way while establishing a climate conducive to positive interactions among students. Research-based programs, such as the *Olweus Bullying Prevention Program,* have proven that schoolwide efforts are more effective in addressing bullying than classroom components alone.

How Can We Address Cyber Bullying on a Schoolwide Level?

The *Cyber Bullying* curriculum should be taught within a school or organizational environment that supports the prevention of all forms of bullying, including cyber bullying, and does not tolerate its existence.

Here are some ways that schools and community organizations can promote and support the message that cyber bullying is not tolerated:

1. Work to create a school environment where respect and responsibility are promoted and bullying is not.

2. Implement a schoolwide program to address bullying of all kinds, such as the *Olweus Bullying Prevention Program,* in conjunction with this classroom curriculum.

3. Set clear school policies about reporting and addressing cyber bullying, whether it occurs on campus or not. (See information about creating school policies on the CD-ROM.)

I-1
through
I-7

4. Train staff to be aware of cyber bullying and to intervene appropriately. A training outline is provided on pages 97–102 in this guide. Have as many staff members as possible complete this training.

5. If a student or parent reports an incident of cyber bullying, take the situation seriously and proactively address the issue, even if the cyber bullying messages did not originate at your school.

6. Establish a no-use policy for cell phones on school grounds, if you don't have one already.

7. Teach the *Cyber Bullying* curriculum to all students. Make program participation mandatory.

I-14

I-15

8. Host a cyber bullying prevention campaign. Involve students in making posters, announcements, and other promotional materials on this important issue. You may also want to use the posters included on the CD-ROM.

9. Make young people aware of the resources in your school and in your community that are available to help them if they experience cyber bullying. Invite community representatives, such as law-enforcement officers, to speak to students about this issue.

10. Involve parents/guardians by hosting parent/guardian education programs, sending home the introductory parent/guardian letter, and using the parent/guardian education resources provided with each lesson in this curriculum.

11. Establish procedures that parents/guardians can follow in reporting cyber bullying incidents to school staff. Make sure parents/guardians and staff know what these procedures are and be sure to proactively address any cyber bullying incidents.

What Resources Are Available Online or in My Community to Help with This Topic?

You don't need to be an expert on cyber bullying to teach this curriculum. However, you may want to turn to community resources for help in presenting this issue or to learn more about it.

Most local law-enforcement agencies can provide guidance on how to address crimes related to cyber bullying. They may also be able to give guidance on how to track the source of anonymous cyber bullying messages.

Also check with local telecommunications companies to see if they have any written materials on cyber technologies that will help you get up to speed on the types of technologies young people are using today.

Pages 103–106 of this curriculum provide a listing of additional resources available to you and for parents as you teach this curriculum.

What Should I Be Aware of When Teaching *Cyber Bullying: A Prevention Curriculum for Grades 3–5?*

Here are some helpful tips on teaching this curriculum:

1. During the first session, it's important to create a sense of trust and safety in your group. Be sure to discuss the need for ground rules (as outlined in session 1). Make sure students abide by these rules throughout the program.

2. When in a group setting, make sure students do not use real names or too many details when describing incidences of cyber bullying that they or others have experienced. Encourage them to share any specific concerns they may have with you in private.

3. Be aware that some students in your class may be experiencing bullying, or cyber bullying in particular. Don't force students to answer questions or talk about their experiences if they're uncomfortable doing so. Also be aware that some students in your class may be bullying others.

4. It's difficult in a class environment to guarantee complete confidentiality. Warn students of this fact, so they don't reveal more than they are comfortable with. Also warn students ahead of time that if they reveal information about someone being hurt by others or someone who is considering hurting himself or herself that you are required to report this information.

5. Maintain respect during discussions. Allow people to offer opposing views, but do so respectfully.

What Are Some Other Guidelines as I Teach *Cyber Bullying: A Prevention Curriculum for Grades 3–5?*

1. *What if a student reveals he or she or a friend is being cyber bullied or bullied in other ways?*

   Before teaching this cyber bullying prevention curriculum, check whether your school has a policy on reporting cyber bullying or bullying of any kind. If you are uncertain about reporting procedures, talk with your school leadership about how incidents should be reported.

   While you are teaching this cyber bullying prevention curriculum, a student may reveal that he or she is either being cyber bullied or is cyber bullying others. As mentioned earlier, it's important at the outset of the program to let students know what you will do upon learning this information, so they don't feel set up or betrayed by the action you take.

   If a student reveals information during a class discussion, do not continue discussing the issue with everyone present. Invite the student to talk privately with you afterward. Write down any information the student provides.

   Don't try to solve this problem on your own. Consult with appropriate school officials and the students' parents or guardians.

2. *What should I do if, while visiting a social-networking Web site, I find examples of cyber bullying among my students?*

   As you become more familiar with cyber technologies that students are using, you may find instances in which students in your school or district are engaged in cyber bullying or other worrisome behavior on the Internet. Whenever possible, print out the information and share it with your school leadership. In most cases, inappropriate information added to social-networking Web sites can be traced back to the person who created it. Often just notifying the parents or guardians of the parties involved may be enough to resolve the situation. However, depending on the seriousness of the issue, you may need to involve law enforcement.

3. *What if parents or guardians are uncomfortable with the topic and don't want their children involved?*

On rare occasions, parents/guardians may express reservations about their child being taught this cyber bullying prevention curriculum. This may be due to the fact that some parents/guardians may not want their child using certain cyber technologies or may be concerned about Internet safety.

While participating in this cyber bullying prevention program, students will not be working online. Care has also been taken to make sure the program does not encourage cyber technology use or give students new ideas on how to cyber bully one another.

In cases where parents/guardians raise concerns, encourage them to review the curriculum. Tell them about the prevalence of cyber bullying among youth and the importance of addressing this issue in a preventative way. Discuss any additional concerns they may have. If parents/guardians still voice reservations, it may be best to have the students complete an alternative project on a related topic.

Be sure to let parents/guardians know about the curriculum in advance through school newsletters or parent nights and by sending home a letter explaining the curriculum. You will find a sample letter on pages 29–31 and the CD-ROM.

Introduction to Cyber Bullying

Jack was in fourth grade. He had an older brother named Nate who was in seventh grade. Nate had just gotten a cell phone, and he had a lot of fun sending text messages to his friends. Sometimes he even let Jack send text messages to their parents' cell phones.

A few months into the school year, Nate wouldn't let Jack even touch his cell phone. And when Nate received text messages on his phone, he would get angry or sometimes not even look at the message. Jack was confused. He thought that Nate loved his phone, and he couldn't understand why Nate seemed not to like it anymore. Nate's grades were also suffering, and he argued with their parents about it.

One evening after supper, Jack accidentally overheard Nate talking to his parents about the mean text messages he was getting from some people at school. He told them that some of his friends were also sending mean messages, and some wouldn't even talk to him anymore. Nate sounded so upset and angry, and he asked his parents what he should do.

Jack was worried about Nate, and he was also worried about getting a cell phone of his own. What if his friends did something like that? At school he looked at his friends and wondered if any of them would send him mean text messages. He was reprimanded by his teacher for not paying attention.

For many students like Jack and Nate, cyber bullying is a serious issue that affects their sense of well-being and their ability to learn in the classroom. In order to understand what cyber bullying is, it is important to first understand what bullying is.

What Is Bullying?

Dan Olweus, Ph.D., a pioneer researcher in the area of bullying, has defined bullying in this way:

> Bullying is when someone repeatedly and on purpose says or does mean or hurtful things to another person who has a hard time defending himself or herself (Olweus, Limber, Flerx, Mullin, Riese, and Snyder 2007).

There are both direct and indirect forms of bullying. More direct forms include physical actions such as hitting someone, taking or damaging someone else's things, or saying mean or hurtful things to someone.

Indirect forms of bullying are more concealed and subtle, and it is more difficult to determine who is causing the bullying. Examples include social exclusion, spreading rumors, and cyber bullying.

Dr. Olweus's research determined that students play a variety of roles in bullying situations. These roles make up what he termed the "Bullying Circle." These roles are diagrammed below.

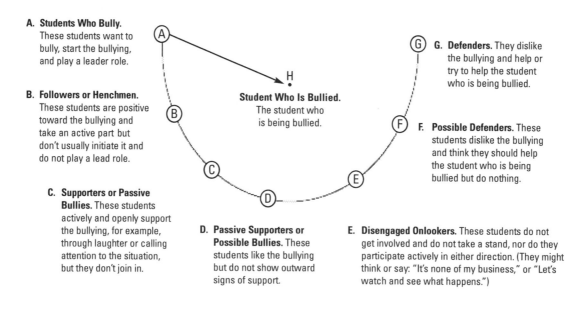

A. Students Who Bully. These students want to bully, start the bullying, and play a leader role.

B. Followers or Henchmen. These students are positive toward the bullying and take an active part but don't usually initiate it and do not play a lead role.

C. Supporters or Passive Bullies. These students actively and openly support the bullying, for example, through laughter or calling attention to the situation, but they don't join in.

D. Passive Supporters or Possible Bullies. These students like the bullying but do not show outward signs of support.

H — Student Who Is Bullied. The student who is being bullied.

E. Disengaged Onlookers. These students do not get involved and do not take a stand, nor do they participate actively in either direction. (They might think or say: "It's none of my business," or "Let's watch and see what happens.")

F. Possible Defenders. These students dislike the bullying and think they should help the student who is being bullied but do nothing.

G. Defenders. They dislike the bullying and help or try to help the student who is being bullied.

The Bullying Circle is taken from Olweus, Dan, Susan P. Limber, Vicki Crocker Flerx, Nancy Mullin, Jane Riese, and Marlene Snyder. 2007. *Olweus bullying prevention program: Teacher guide.* Center City, MN: Hazelden Publishing.

In effective bullying prevention efforts, it is helpful to focus on changing the attitudes and behaviors of the bystanders, who generally make up 80 percent of a school's student body. The goal is to move these bystanders into the position of defending or helping the student who is being bullied. This is a primary goal of *Cyber Bullying: A Prevention Curriculum for Grades 3–5.*

What Is Cyber Bullying?

Cyber bullying is bullying through email, instant messaging, in a chat room, on a Web site, or through digital messages or images sent to a cellular phone or personal digital assistant (PDA) (Kowalski et al. 2008). Cyber bullying, like traditional bullying, involves a negative action that is often repeated and involves an imbalance of power.

In traditional forms of bullying, individuals may have more power over another by being bigger, stronger, or more popular. With cyber bullying, an individual may have more power just by being able to instantly share negative comments or photographs with a multitude of people via email, instant messaging, text messaging, or through Web site posts. Cyber bullying may also involve several individuals targeting one individual or a more popular student targeting a less popular classmate.

Traditional bullying is also defined by mean or negative actions being repeated and occurring over time. When someone is cyber bullied, this repetition of negative behavior can occur by sending one embarrassing photo or one degrading email message, which may in turn be forwarded to an entire class or grade level. The perpetrator, while usually known in a traditional bullying situation, might go unidentified in the case of cyber bullying.

Traditional bullying usually occurs in a certain time and space, perhaps during school in the bathrooms or the hallways. Students who are bullied can usually find some relief at home or away from school. When a student is cyber bullied, the incident can happen whenever someone turns on his or her computer or accesses the Internet. This often happens at home at any time of the day or night.

Cyber bullying poses unique challenges because it frequently happens outside the school setting, and thus may be difficult for educators to observe. In addition, students may feel invisible or anonymous while accessing the Internet, which may lead to a greater willingness to engage in negative actions. Finally, without

Duplicating this page is illegal. Do not copy this material without written permission from the publisher.

11

face-to-face interaction, students who cyber bully have no opportunity to witness the emotional distress their comments may be inflicting on a peer.

There is a bright spot, however. While direct evidence may be hard to obtain in many traditional forms of bullying, cyber bullying typically involves a form of communication that can be saved and printed from a computer or saved on a cell phone. Such obvious evidence can be helpful when intervening in cyber bullying incidents.

What Are the Warning Signs of Cyber Bullying?

The warning signs of cyber bullying are similar to those of traditional bullying in terms of emotional effects; however, there are some differences. For example, we would not expect to see bruises or torn clothing on a child who is being cyber bullied. However, it is also important to keep in mind that some students who are cyber bullied may also be experiencing traditional bullying at school.

A student may be experiencing cyber bullying if he or she

- appears sad, moody, or anxious
- avoids school
- withdraws from or shows a lack of interest in social activities
- experiences a drop in grades or a decline in academic performance
- appears upset after using the computer or being online
- appears upset after viewing a text message

If a student shows any of these warning signs, it is important to talk with the student and investigate the student's online presence to determine if cyber bullying is occurring and to offer help where needed.

Why Should Schools Address the Issue of Cyber Bullying?

Schools have rapidly embraced technology due to its ability to offer advanced learning opportunities and resources to students. Teachers use blogs, students post assignments online, and some schools issue laptops and PDAs to students as instructional tools. By embracing technology and encouraging students to explore its various forms, educators also have a duty to teach students to use such technologies in a responsible manner.

In addition, many schools are already adopting comprehensive bullying prevention programs, such as the *Olweus Bullying Prevention Program,* or are at least teaching classroom lessons that address bullying behaviors. Cyber bullying is one form of bullying that should be specifically addressed as part of these comprehensive efforts.

Research has shown that not all students perceive cyber bullying as a form of bullying behavior (Kowalski et al. 2008). Therefore, classroom lessons and discussions that focus directly on cyber bullying are critical to prevent it from flourishing.

What Is the Prevalence of Cyber Bullying?

While the numbers vary based on the methods used to gather the data, the Pew Internet Survey found that almost one-third of teens had experienced cyber bullying (Lenhart 2007). In addition, Kowalski and Limber (2007) found that 22 percent of middle school students had some form of involvement in cyber bullying (defined as being cyber bullied or cyber bullying others at least once in the previous couple of months). Thus, high percentages of students are affected by this behavior. Without specific prevention efforts, the numbers will likely increase as more students become "wired" at increasingly younger ages.

How Is Cyber Bullying Affecting Students, Schools, and Communities?

Current research demonstrates that students who are targets of traditional bullying are more likely to have low self-esteem (Olweus 1993; Rigby and Slee 1993), be anxious and depressed (Juvonen, Graham, and Schuster 2003), and experience a variety of health problems such as stomachaches, headaches, fatigue, and difficulty sleeping and eating (Fekkes, Pijpers, and Verloove-VanHorick 2004) than students not involved with traditional bullying. They also are more likely to have thoughts of suicide (Rigby 1997). Students who are afraid to come to school and are being targeted by peer abuse such as cyber bullying are not likely to give their full attention to academics. Students who are bullied have higher absenteeism rates and lower grades than students who are not bullied (Arseneault et al. 2006; Eisenberg, Neumark-Sztainer, and Perry 2003; Rigby 1997).

Research on cyber bullying specifically suggests that students involved in cyber bullying (particularly those who are cyber bullied and who also cyber bully others) are more likely to be anxious, to be depressed, and to have lower self-esteem than students who are not involved (Kowalski et al. 2008). Students who are cyber bullied are also more likely to have lower grades and higher absenteeism rates than those students not involved (Kowalski et al. 2008).

Although cyber bullying usually occurs outside of the school day, it can impact school when students are afraid to face their peer group after receiving mean comments or messages at home. In addition, many students are targets of traditional bullying at school and cyber bullying at home, which can leave them feeling that there is no safe haven available to them.

Educators and administrators frequently observe that investigating and intervening in cyber bullying incidents can be very time-consuming. Parents also report feeling victimized when their children are targeted by cyber bullying (Kowalski et al. 2008). Just as schools discuss character education for the real world, they need to discuss how students treat one another in the online world as technology advances.

What Should Teachers Do if They Know or Suspect Cyber Bullying Is Occurring?

It is important to educate students about how to report all forms of bullying, including cyber bullying, to adults at school and at home. This should be part of the teacher's ongoing classroom discussions about bullying. Session 5 in the curriculum also teaches students these skills.

If a teacher suspects a student is being cyber bullied, he or she should advise the student to ask his or her parents or guardians to help. The teacher can also show the student how to save any evidence of the cyber bullying and report it by using a copy of the printed online communications as evidence. The student can bring the evidence to the teacher, a school counselor, or an administrator. If there is no evidence, the student should still report the cyber bullying and include a description of what is taking place so that a counselor or administrator can investigate and speak with the parties involved.

Although all adults at school should have an understanding of cyber bullying and should be open to receiving reports of cyber bullying, it will be most helpful if there are identified individuals at each school who are particularly knowledgeable about bullying and cyber bullying. These individuals will want to investigate and determine if there is any on-campus traditional bullying and/or cyber bullying accompanying off-campus cyber bullying.

Any evidence of bullying at school should be addressed with consistent consequences for the student engaged in bullying behavior and with heightened adult supervision around the targeted student. In addition, positive bystanders should be encouraged to support the targeted student through a variety of means such as those suggested in this curriculum. Check with your school administrators to determine the appropriate person to whom cyber bullying incidents should be reported.

Some forms of cyber bullying are illegal. Educators should always contact law enforcement if communications involve death threats, extortion, intimidation, or threats based on race, religion, gender, or sexual orientation, and any evidence of sexual exploitation (Kowalski et al. 2008; Willard 2007). See the CD-ROM for additional guidance about legal issues and cyber bullying.

I-1 through I-3

If the cyber bullying takes place off campus, does not potentially violate the law, and is not accompanied by on-campus bullying, educators may be somewhat more limited in the actions they can take (e.g., sanctions may violate a student's First Amendment rights). But they can still take steps to intervene by conferencing separately with the students involved and their parents. Teachers can try to monitor any interactions between the involved students more closely, or perhaps they can change class schedules to minimize the contact between the students. They can advise the student who is bullied to save the evidence in case the situation escalates. School counselors might also get involved by arranging a meeting between the students to resolve the situation, although care must be taken in doing so (see Kowalski, Limber, and Agatston 2008 for a discussion of these sensitive situations). Educators can also assist the parents or guardians of a targeted student by providing educational literature on preventing and responding to cyber bullying, as well as giving them information on how to report offensive profiles to social-networking sites. This educational literature is provided on the curriculum CD-ROM.

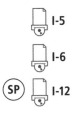
I-5

I-6

SP I-12

Session	Student Learner Outcomes	Parent/Guardian Learner Outcomes
Session 1: **What Is Bullying?**	*Students will* • Define *bullying*. • Identify examples of bullying. • Identify some of the roles students play in the "Bullying Circle." • Identify rules to prevent bullying.	*Parents/guardians will* • Describe the definition of *bullying* and why it's different from playful teasing. • Explain how prevalent bullying is. • Know why it's important to intervene and how to do that.
Session 2: **What Is Cyber Bullying?**	*Students will* • Define *cyber bullying*. • Identify examples of cyber bullying. • Understand the importance of not sharing passwords.	*Parents/guardians will* • Explain the definition of *cyber bullying*. • List the different technologies that their children will eventually be using. • Describe how to show their child how important it is that only they and their child know their child's password (Internet safety). • Explain how prevalent and serious cyber bullying can become.
Session 3: **How Does Cyber Bullying Affect People?**	*Students will* • Identify the effects of cyber bullying. • Empathize with people who are cyber bullied.	*Parents/guardians will* • Know that though most cyber bullying happens outside school, it does have ramifications in school. • Explain the social and emotional harm cyber bullying can inflict. • Describe what some of the academic consequences of cyber bullying can be. • Know that they have control over their children's online activities.

Session	Student Learner Outcomes	Parent/Guardian Learner Outcomes
Session 4: **How Do I Treat People Well When I Use Technology?**	*Students will* • Define what *netiquette* is. • Identify basic rules of netiquette for online communication.	*Parents/guardians will* • Know basic online courtesy, or *netiquette*. • Know how important family rules are regarding the Internet, cell phones, cameras, and instant messaging.
Session 5: **What Do I Do if Someone Is Mean to Me through Technology?**	*Students will* • Identify possible responses to cyber bullying situations. • Know that part of being safe online means telling an adult if they experience cyber bullying. • Explain how telling an adult when they or someone they know is being cyber bullied is not "tattling."	*Parents/guardians will* • Explain what their options are if their child is cyber bullied. • Describe what they can do if their child's friend is cyber bullied. • Explain how cyber bullying others and being cyber bullied can affect their child's online reputation. • Describe how research shows that children don't tell about cyber bullying for fear of losing cell phone and Internet privileges. Know not to make that a consequence.

Related National Academic Standards

Using *Cyber Bullying: A Prevention Curriculum for Grades 3–5* will help you meet the following national academic standards:

Health Education Standards[1]

Students in grades 3–5 will

- identify how peers can influence healthy and unhealthy behaviors

- explain how media influences thoughts, feelings, and behaviors

- describe ways that technology can influence personal health

- demonstrate effective verbal and nonverbal communication skills to enhance health

- demonstrate refusal skills that avoid or reduce health risks

- demonstrate how to ask for assistance to enhance personal health

- demonstrate a variety of behaviors that avoid or reduce health risks

- encourage others to make positive health choices

---

1. Joint Committee on National Health Education Standards, *National Health Education Standards, Second Edition, Achieving Excellence,* The American Cancer Society, 2007.

Technology Education Standards[2]

Communication and Collaboration

Students in grades 3–5 will

- interact, collaborate, and publish with peers, experts, or others employing a variety of digital environments and media

- communicate information and ideas effectively to multiple audiences using a variety of media and formats

- contribute to project teams to produce original works or solve problems

Critical Thinking, Problem-Solving, and Decision-Making

Students in grades 3–5 will

- identify and define authentic problems and significant questions for investigation

- plan and manage activities to develop a solution or complete a project

- collect and analyze data to identify solutions and/or make informed decisions

- use multiple processes and diverse perspectives to explore alternative solutions

Digital Citizenship

Students in grades 3–5 will

- advocate and practice safe, legal, and responsible use of information and technology

- exhibit a positive attitude toward using technology that supports collaboration, learning, and productivity

- demonstrate personal responsibility for lifelong learning

- exhibit leadership for digital citizenship

---

2. *National Educational Technology Standards for Students, Second Edition,* © 2007, ISTE® (International Society for Technology in Education), www.iste.org. All rights reserved.

Session Description and Preparation

Here is an overview of the preparation you'll need to do to teach each *Cyber Bullying* session.

Session Title	Session Description	Materials Needed	Preparation Needed
Session 1: What Is Bullying?	Through a story, a large-group discussion, and a creative rap activity, students will define *bullying* and the *Bullying Circle*, and identify rules to prevent bullying.	• CD-ROM materials 　– Parent/Guardian Letter 　*(ALSO ON PAGES 29–31 OF MANUAL)* 　📄 I-10 (SP) 　– Glossary of Cyber Terms 　*(ALSO ON PAGES 33–36 OF MANUAL)* 　📄 I-11 (SP) 　– Internet Safety Tips for Parents and Guardians 　*(ALSO ON PAGES 37–40 OF MANUAL)* 　📄 I-12 (SP) 　– Session 1: The Story 　📄 S1-1 　– The Bullying Circle diagram 📄 S1-2 　– The Four Anti-Bullying Rules sheet 📄 S1-3 　– Homework Assignment 1 　📄 S1-4 (SP) • Overhead projector or a computer and LCD projector • Transparency sheets (if using an overhead projector) • Paper and pencils	• Print out, copy, and send the Parent/Guardian Letter, the Glossary of Cyber Terms, and the Internet Safety Tips for Parents and Guardians home with each student prior to starting the program. • Print out and copy the Session 1: The Story handout, one per student. • Print out and copy the Bullying Circle diagram and the Four Anti-Bullying Rules sheet onto transparency sheets if using an overhead projector. If using an LCD projector, have the CD-ROM documents ready to show. • Print out and copy Homework Assignment 1, one per student.

Session Title	Session Description	Materials Needed	Preparation Needed

Session 2: What Is Cyber Bullying?	Through a story, a large-group discussion, and a game, students will understand what cyber bullying is and recognize cyber bullying situations. They will also understand the importance of keeping their computer password, if they have one, a secret.	• CD-ROM materials
		  – Session 2: The Story S2-1
		  – Cyber Bullying HURTS poster I-14
		  – Know It Show It Situations S2-2
		  – Know It Show It Game Sheet S2-3
		  – Know It Show It Game Answer Sheet S2-4
		  – Homework Assignment 2 S2-5 (SP)
		• Pencils
			• Print out and copy the Session 2: The Story handout, one per student.
			• Print out the poster. Enlarge and hang it up in your classroom where students can see it.
			• Print out and copy the Know It Show It Game Sheet, one per student team.
			• Print out and copy Homework Assignment 2, one per student.

Session 3: How Does Cyber Bullying Affect People?	Through a story and a large-group discussion, students will understand how cyber bullying affects the student who is bullied, the student who bullies others, and bystanders. Through an active game, students will have an opportunity to react empathetically to a variety of situations.	• CD-ROM materials
		  – Session 3: The Story S3-1
		  – Technology Ups and Downs Activity Situations S3-2
		  – Homework Assignment 3 S3-3 (SP)
		• Cyber Bullying HURTS poster (used in session 2)
			• Print out and copy the Session 3: The Story handout, one per student.
			• Print out the Technology Ups and Downs Activity Situations.
			• Print out and copy Homework Assignment 3, one per student.
			• Hang the Cyber Bullying HURTS poster in a place where students can see it.

Session Title	Session Description	Materials Needed	Preparation Needed
Session 4: How Do I Treat People Well When I Use Technology?	Through a story, a large-group discussion, and the creation of posters, students will learn the basic rules of netiquette.	• CD-ROM materials – Session 4: The Story 📄 **S4-1** – Netta-Kit poster 📄 **I-15** – Homework Assignment 4 📄 **S4-2** (SP) • Pencils • Construction paper • Crayons or markers	• Print out and copy the Session 4: The Story handout, one per student. • Print out, enlarge, and hang the Netta-Kit poster. • Print out and copy Homework Assignment 4, one per student.
Session 5: What Do I Do if Someone Is Mean to Me through Technology?	Through a story, a large-group discussion, and a class game, students will learn what they can do if they or someone they know is cyber bullied.	• CD-ROM materials – Session 5: The Story 📄 **S5-1** – TELL KIDS TELL handout 📄 **S5-2** – Who Got the Message? Game Squares 📄 **S5-3** – Who Got the Message? Messages 📄 **S5-4** – Homework Assignment 5 📄 **S5-5** (SP) • Overhead projector or LCD projector • Netta-Kit poster (used in session 4) • Pencils • CD player or some music source that can be turned on and off • Transparency sheets (if using overhead projector)	• Print out and copy the Session 5: The Story handout, one per student. • If using an overhead projector, print out and copy TELL KIDS TELL onto transparency sheets. If using an LCD projector, have the CD-ROM document ready to show. • Print out, copy, and cut out the Who Got the Message? Game Squares, one square per student. • Print out one copy of the Who Got the Message? Messages. • Cue the music on the CD player and have that ready to go. • Print out and copy Homework Assignment 5, one per student.

Cyber Bullying Pre-test/Post-test

Name _____

Teacher_____

Write your answers in the spaces provided.

1. What is the definition of *bullying?*

   _____

   _____

   _____

   _____

2. List three roles people could play in the Bullying Circle.

   a. _____

   b. _____

   c. _____

3. List two ways that cyber bullying might be different from being bullied at school.

   a. _____

   b. _____

4. How might being cyber bullied make someone feel? List two ways.

a. _____

b. _____

5. List three things you could do if you were cyber bullied.

a. _____

b. _____

c. _____

Write "T" for true or "F" for false on the line in front of each statement below.

_____ 6. Cyber bullying only happens through the Internet.

_____ 7. It's okay to share your password with your friends if you really trust them.

_____ 8. "Netiquette" is how you treat someone when you're playing a sport that has nets.

_____ 9. Everything that is done on a computer is recorded inside of it.

_____ 10. It's important to save the evidence if you are cyber bullied.

Answers for the Pre-test/Post-test

1. Bullying is when someone repeatedly and on purpose says or does mean or hurtful things to another person who has a hard time defending himself or herself.

2. Possible answers include

   - person who is bullied

   - person who is bullying someone

   - followers of the person who is doing the bullying who join in after it starts

   - supporters of the person who is doing the bullying who don't join in but encourage or laugh at the bullying

   - passive supporters who like the bullying but don't show it

   - onlookers who don't have a positive or negative reaction

   - possible defenders who don't like the bullying and think they should do something about it but do nothing

   - defenders who try to help the person who is being bullied

3. Possible answers include

   - Cyber bullying can reach and involve many people very quickly.

   - People who might not bully someone to his or her face might cyber bully someone because they can't be seen and can be anonymous.

   - Traditional forms of bullying can cause physical harm and psychological harm, while in most cases cyber bullying causes psychological harm.

   - Traditional bullying is usually limited to the people in the immediate area where the bullying is taking place. Cyber bullying can reach many people immediately—and often these people are not even known to the target.

   - Traditional bullying usually has a time and place, such as the school playground at recess. Cyber bullying can happen anytime and anyplace. The target may even be unaware that it is happening for a while.

   - It is usually apparent who is doing traditional bullying. It is often difficult to find out who is doing cyber bullying.

4. Children who are cyber bullied might

   a. feel sad, upset, scared, nervous, worried

   b. feel like they don't want to go to school

   c. not like themselves very much

   d. sometimes lose friends because of the bullying

5. Possible answers include ignore it, block the sender, tell an adult, respond but not retaliate, trace the sender, contact the Internet Service Provider or social-networking site, and save the evidence.

6. False

7. False

8. False

9. True

10. True

Parent/Guardian Letter

Dear Parent/Guardian,

Our class will be taking part in a cyber bullying prevention curriculum. Cyber bullying is bullying through email, Web sites (such as social-networking sites), chat rooms, instant messaging, and cell phones. You may have heard about cyber bullying in the news recently. It has become an important issue for many youth and their families. As Internet and cell phone use have become an integral part of our daily lives, abuses of these technologies have also grown.

This cyber bullying prevention curriculum includes five sessions designed to teach students how to recognize cyber bullying, how cyber bullying affects students and the school community, what to do if cyber bullying happens to them or to people they know, and how to prevent it from happening.

Students will be engaged in classroom discussions, small-group activities, and projects to gain an understanding of how cell phones, text messaging, instant messaging, Web sites, and email can be abused, and what they can do about it. Students will identify how to use the Internet and cell phones in positive ways. They will also be encouraged to develop a sense of empathy for students who are bullied in the traditional sense and/or cyber bullied.

Cyber bullying is a matter that concerns us at school and is also a matter that should be discussed at home. There is a parent/guardian component to this program. I hope you will take the time to read the materials that will be brought home and to do the homework activities with your child. Included in this homework are some Web sites that you and your child could visit together to learn more about what you can do to increase Internet safety and prevent cyber bullying. Your child will be graded on these homework assignments, so be sure to sign them when completed and return them to class.

Please feel free to contact me if you have any questions about this program.

Sincerely,

Duplicating this page for personal or group use is permissible.

29

Carta para el padre o tutor

Estimado Padre/Tutor,

Nuestra clase estará participando en un programa de prevención de la ciber-intimidación. La ciber-intimidación es intimidar a través del correo electrónico, de sitios Web, como sitios de redes sociales, foros de charla (*chat rooms*), mensajes instántáneos y teléfonos móviles. Es posible que últimamente usted haya oido hablar en las noticias sobre la ciber-intimidación. Se ha convertido en un tema importante para muchos jóvenes y sus familias. Al mismo tiempo que el Internet y el teléfono móvil se han hecho una parte integral de nuestras vidas diarias, también ha crecido el abuso de esas tecnologías.

Este programa de prevención de la ciber-intimidación incluye cinco sesiones diseñadas para enseñar a los estudiantes cómo reconocer la ciber-intimidación, cómo afecta a los estudiantes y a la comunidad escolar, qué pueden hacer si les ocurre a ellos o a personas que conozcan, y de cómo prevenir que ocurra la ciber-intimidación.

Los estudiantes se involucrarán en discusiones en clase y en actividades de grupos pequeños y proyectos para entender cómo los teléfonos móviles, mensajes de texto, mensajes instántáneos, sitios Web, y el correo electrónico pueden abusarse, y qué pueden hacer al respecto. Los estudiantes identificarán formas positivas de usar el Internet y el teléfono móvil. Además se les animará a desarrollar su sentido de empatía por los estudiantes intimidados en el sentido tradicional o ciber-intimidados.

La ciber-intimidación es un tema que nos preocupa en la escuela y además es algo que debe hablarse en el hogar. En este programa existe un componente para los padres/tutores. Espero que usted se tome el tiempo para leer los materiales que su hijo/a traerá al hogar y hacer las actividades junto con él o ella. Se incluyen en esta tarea algunos sitios Web que usted y su hijo/a pueden visitar juntos para conocer más sobre lo qué pueden hacer para incrementar la seguridad en el Internet y para prevenir la ciber-intimidación. Su hijo/a recibirá calificaciones por esas tareas, así que asegúrese de firmarlas cuando las complete, y las devuelva a la clase.

Quedo a su disposición si tuviera preguntas sobre este programa.

Atentamente,

Glossary of Cyber Terms

blog: An abbreviation for Web log. A blog is a Web site where entries are typically written in chronological order and may function as commentary, news, or an online diary. Many blogs include a place for viewers to post comments.

chat room: A Web site or online space where people can communicate in real time. Chat rooms are usually organized around specific topics or interests.

email: Electronic mail. Email is used to send messages (usually in text form) from one Internet user to another.

emoticon: A symbol used to express emotions in electronic forms of communication, such as ☺ or ☹.

flaming: Sending rude or threatening messages, usually on discussion boards, in chat rooms, and through email.

instant messaging (IMing): A tool for communicating that combines the real-time features of chat rooms with the person-to-person contact of email. Internet service providers (see entry below) may provide free instant messaging services, or the software may be downloaded from the Internet.

Internet: Vast networks of computers connected throughout the world that allow users to share information through email, online chat rooms, file transfers, and Web pages.

Internet service provider (ISP): Any company that provides access to the Internet. America Online (AOL) and Comcast are two examples.

message board: A Web site with a submission form that allows users to post messages for others to read and respond to. These messages (called "threads") are usually sorted within discussion categories or topics.

netiquette: A contraction of the words *net* and *etiquette* that refers to the online code of manners for using the Internet. For example, it is considered rude to post a message in all capital letters because it implies shouting.

social-networking Web site (SNS): Web sites on which users can create profiles and develop networks that connect them to other users. Some sites are built around a common interest, and others are mainly social in nature. These sites allow users to share information about themselves and to communicate with other users through forums, chat rooms, emails, or instant messaging.

text messaging or short message system (SMS): A means of sending short messages to and from mobile phones. Because text messages are typed on a phone keypad, most messages are abbreviations and symbols.

video-sharing Web sites: Sites that allow users to upload and share videos that users have created or found. Most sites allow users to rate or comment on the videos that are posted. YouTube.com is an example of a video-sharing site.

Glosario de cibervocablos

blog: Una abreviatura de Web log. Un "blog" o bitácora es un sitio Web donde se escriben artículos o texto, típicamente en orden cronológico, y que pueden actuar como comentarios, noticias, o como un diario en línea. Muchos "blogs" incluyen un lugar para que los lectores publiquen comentarios.

chat room: Un sitio Web o un espacio en línea, donde las personas pueden comunicarse en tiempo real. Normalmente los *chat rooms* o foros de charla están organizados por temas e intereses específicos.

email: Correo electrónico. Se usa para enviar mensajes (normalmente en forma de texto) de un usuario de Internet a otro.

emoticon: Un símbolo que expresa emociones en formas electrónicas de comunicación, como ☺ o ☹.

flaming: Enviar mensajes groseros o amenazantes, normalmente en foros de discusión, foros de charla, y a través del correo electrónico.

instant messaging (IMing): La mensajería instantánea es una herramienta de comunicación que combina características de tiempo real en foros de charla con contacto de persona a persona a través del correo electrónico. Los proveedores de servicios de Internet (ver definición a continuación) pueden ofrecer servicios gratis de mensajería instantánea, o "bajar" el software desde el Internet.

Internet: Redes inmensas de computadoras conectadas en todo el mundo, que permiten a los usuarios compartir información a través del correo electrónico, foros de charla en línea, transferencia de archivos, y páginas Web.

Internet service provider (ISP): Es una compañía que provee servicios de acceso al Internet. América Online (AOL) y Comcast son dos ejemplos.

message board: Un sitio Web, como si fuera un tablero electrónico de anuncios con un formulario que permite a los usuarios publicar mensajes para que otras personas puedan leerlos y responderlos. Generalmente, estos mensajes se dividen por categorías o tópicos de discusión.

netiqueta: La contracción de las palabras *net y iqueta* (normas de etiqueta) que se refiere al código de modales en línea para usar el Internet. Por ejemplo, se considera grosero publicar un mensaje con todas las letras en mayúscula dado que da la impresión de estar gritando.

social-networking Web sites (SNS): Sitios Web en los que los usuarios pueden crear perfiles personales y desarrollar redes que los conectan a otros usuarios. Algunos sitios se construyen alrededor de un interés común, y otros son principalmente de caracter social. Estos sitios permiten a los usuarios compartir información sobre ellos y comunicarse con otros usuarios a través de los foros, foros de charla, correo electrónico, o mensaje instantáneo.

text messaging o short message system (SMS): Una forma de enviar mensajes cortos a y desde los teléfonos móviles. Dado que los mensajes de texto se ingresan con el teclado pequeño del telefóno, la mayoría de ellos son abreviaturas y símbolos.

video sharing Web sites: Son sitios que permiten a los usuarios "subir" y compartir videos que ellos han creado o encontrado. La mayoría de los sitios permiten a los usuarios de valorar o comentar sobre los videos que se publiquen. YouTube.com es un ejemplo de un sitio para compartir videos.

Internet Safety Tips for Parents and Guardians

The most important thing you can do is *teach* your children appropriate use of computers and cell phones. Make sure they know to tell you if they receive an inappropriate message or photo. There are other ways to help limit your child's access to Web sites and computer use:

- Take advantage of free parental controls and spam blockers provided by your Internet service provider. Set your search engine's preferences to "strict filtering" to avoid inappropriate content.

- Bookmark appropriate sites for your children to visit and make a rule that these are the only sites they can visit online. If they want to visit a new site, they must check with you first.

- Teach your children to use a kid-friendly search engine like Yahooligans. Find out what search engine they use at school.

- Limit your children's online time to one hour or less a day.

- As your children move into the tween and teen years, consider adding monitoring software. Monitoring software allows you to view the sites your children are visiting and also allows you to review chat sessions and comments they are posting on social-networking sites. You can also view the history of sites visited. (Children often learn how to delete this information, however.)

- Discuss what information is appropriate to share online and what information is too private or personal. Make sure your children know to avoid posting their phone number, cell phone number, date of birth, or home address on Web sites or in instant messages.

- Make rules about sharing and sending photos. Younger children should only do this with your permission. Discuss whom children can share photos with and what types of photos are appropriate. If your children are posting photos on a social-networking site, make sure that they use a privacy feature that only allows their friends to view their photographs.

- Make sure children know to keep their password private.

- Online friends should be friends in the real world. Friends on their buddy lists and social-networking sites should be people they know, rather than friends of friends.

- Keep the computer in a central place where you can observe what your children are doing. Computers and laptops should not be in bedrooms if they have Internet capability.

- Install antivirus software on your computer and keep it up-to-date. Use a firewall for protection. Children are notorious for downloading games and applications from Web sites that may include harmful viruses. Make sure you back up files regularly.

- Teach your children how to communicate appropriately in cyberspace. Explain how easy it is for messages to be misinterpreted online. Discuss the golden rule as it applies to cyberspace. Stress to your children: "If you wouldn't want someone to say that to you, don't send it in a message." Discuss how easily rumors get started online and the importance of avoiding gossip. Teach your children how to be rumor blockers (don't pass it on) rather than rumor starters. Remind them not to respond to a message if they are feeling angry or upset. It's okay to respond after they have calmed down.

- Respect the minimum age guidelines of social-networking sites. Do not allow your children to lie about their age to bypass the age limits. If you are willing to let your children have profiles on social-networking sites such as MySpace or Facebook, set them up together. Emphasize how important it is for you to know their passwords.

- Search the Internet for your children's names, screen names, phone numbers, and address regularly to see what pops up. Teach him or her the importance of building a positive online reputation for the future, as employers and colleges may search for information about them online.

Consejos para los padres y tutores sobre la seguridad en el uso del Internet

Lo más importante que usted puede hacer es enseñar a sus hijos acerca del uso debido de las computadoras y de los teléfonos móviles. Asegúrese que ellos sepan que pueden venir a contarle cuando reciban mensajes o fotos inapropiados. Además existen otras formas de ayudar a limitar el acceso del niño a los sitios Web y al uso de la computadora:

- Aprovéchese de los controles gratis para los padres y los bloqueadores de *spam* ofrecidos por su proveedor de servicios de Internet. Configure sus preferencias de motores de búsqueda para tener un "filtro específico" que evita recibir contenido indebido.

- Marque los sitios apropiados que sus hijos pueden visitar, y establezca la regla que esos son los únicos sitios que pueden visitar en línea. Si desean visitar otro sitio, deben preguntarle a usted primero.

- Enseñe a sus hijos a usar un motor de búsqueda apropiado para su edad como Yahooligans. Averigue qué motor de búsqueda usa en la escuela.

- Limite el tiempo que sus hijos están en línea, a una hora o menos al dia.

- A medida que sus hijos pasan de la pre adolescencia a la adolescencia considere agregar software de monitoreo en su computadora. El software de monitoreo le permite ver los sitios que sus hijos frecuentas y además examinar las sesiones de charla y los comentarios que estén publicando en los sitios de red social. Usted también puede ver el historial de los sitios visitados. (Sin embargo, los niños saben cómo borrar esta información.)

- Hable sobre qué información es apropiada de compartir en línea y qué información es muy privada o personal. Asegúrese que sus hijos sepan cómo evitar publicar su número de teléfono fijo, su número de teléfono móvil, fecha de nacimiento, o la dirección de su casa en los sitios Web o en mensajes instantáneos.

- Establezca reglas para compartir y enviar fotografías. Los niños más jóvenes deben hacer esto sólo con su permiso. Hablen con quién pueden compartir fotografías y qué tipos de fotografías son apropiados. Si sus hijos están publicando fotografías en un sitio de red social, asegúrese que usan una función de privacidad que sólo permite a sus amigos ver sus fotografías.

- Asegúrese que los hijos sepan cómo mantener confidencial su contraseña.

- Los amigos en línea deben ser amigos en el mundo real. Los amigos en sus listas de amigos cercanos y los sitios de red social deben ser personas que conozcan, y no amigos de amigos.

- Coloque la computadora en un lugar central donde usted pueda observar lo que hacen sus niños. Las computadoras y los laptops no deben estar en los dormitorios si ellos tienen acceso al Internet.

- Instale software antivirus en su computadora y manténgalo actualizado. Use un "firewall" o barrera de protección. Es muy común que los niños "bajen" juegos y aplicaciones de sitios Web que pueden contener virus dañinos. Asegúrese de hacer copias regularmente de los archivos.

- Instruya a sus hijos de cómo comunicarse debidamente en el ciberespacio. Explíquele lo fácil que es que los mensajes sean malentendidos en línea. Hable sobre la "regla de oro" cuando se trata del ciber-espacio. Enfatice a sus hijos que: "Si no quieres que alguien diga eso de ti, no lo envíes en un mensaje." Comente lo fácil que es empezar rumores en línea y la importancia de evitar los chismes. Enseñe a sus hijos cómo ser bloqueadores de rumores (no diseminarlos) en lugar de ser iniciadores de rumores. Recuérdeles de no responder a un mensaje si están enfadados o disgustados. Está bien responder después de calmarse.

- Respete las reglas de edad mínima de los sitios de red social. No permita a sus hijos de mentir sobre su edad para pasar por alto los límites de edad. Si usted está dispuesto a permitir a sus hijos de tener un perfil personal en un sitio de red social como MySpace o Facebook, prepárenlo juntos. Recalque lo importante que es para usted saber sus contraseñas.

- Busque regularmente en el Internet los nombres de sus hijos, nombres de pantalla, números de teléfono, y direcciones para ver lo que aparece. Enséñeles la importancia de tener una reputación positiva en línea para el futuro, dado que los empleadores y universidades pueden buscar información sobre ellos en línea.

The Sessions

What Is Bullying?

Description*

Through a story, a large-group discussion, and a creative rap activity, students will define bullying and the "Bullying Circle," and identify rules to prevent bullying.

* If schools are already implementing the *Olweus Bullying Prevention Program,* teachers may want to abbreviate information covered in session 1. If bullying is a new topic of discussion, teachers may need to extend this discussion.

Student Learner Outcomes

By the end of this session, students will be able to

- define bullying

- identify examples of bullying

- identify some of the roles students play in the "Bullying Circle"

- identify rules to prevent bullying

Parent/Guardian Learner Outcomes

By reading the session 1 information and completing Homework Assignment 1 with their child, parents and guardians will be able to

- describe the definition of bullying and why it's different from playful teasing

---

**SESSION 1
AT A GLANCE**

Total Time: 40 minutes

Part 1:
Program
Introduction
(20 minutes)

Part 2:
Creating
Rule Raps
(15 minutes)

Part 3:
Conclusion
and Homework
Assignment
(5 minutes)

- explain how prevalent bullying is

- know why it's important to intervene and how to do that

Materials Needed

☐ CD-ROM materials

- Parent/Guardian Letter ⬚ I-10 (SP) *(also on pages 29–31 of this manual)*

- Glossary of Cyber Terms ⬚ I-11 (SP) *(also on pages 33–36 of this manual)*

- Internet Safety Tips for Parents and
  Guardians ⬚ I-12 (SP) *(also on pages 37–40 of this manual)*

- Session 1: The Story ⬚ S1-1

- The Bullying Circle diagram ⬚ S1-2

- The Four Anti-Bullying Rules sheet ⬚ S1-3

- Homework Assignment 1 ⬚ S1-4 (SP)

☐ overhead projector or a computer and LCD projector

☐ transparency sheets (if using an overhead projector)

☐ paper and pencils

Preparation Needed

1. Print out, copy, and send the Parent/Guardian Letter, the Glossary of Cyber Terms, and the Internet Safety Tips for Parents and Guardians home with each student prior to starting the program.

2. Print out and copy the Session 1: The Story handout, one per student.

3. Print out and copy the Bullying Circle diagram and Four Anti-Bullying Rules sheet onto transparency sheets if using an overhead projector. If using an LCD projector, have the CD-ROM documents ready to show.

4. Print out and copy Homework Assignment 1, one per student.

SESSION **1** OUTLINE

PART 1
20 minutes

▶ **Program Introduction**

The purpose of part 1 is to introduce *Cyber Bullying: A Prevention Curriculum for Grades 3–5* and read the first story to define bullying, the Bullying Circle, and the Four Anti-Bullying Rules.

1. Explain to the students:

   Today we are going to start a program about cyber bullying. You may or may not know what cyber bullying is, but you probably know what bullying is. You might know a lot about bullying or you might not know very much. To know what cyber bullying is, you have to know what bullying is. This is what we will be talking about today.

   During this program, we'll be reading some stories about two 5th graders named Texter and Internetta. Those sure are interesting names! You'll find out how they got their names in today's story.

Hi, I'm Texter!

Hi, I'm Internetta!

2. Hand out the story for session 1 to each student. Read the story aloud or call on students to read the story aloud while the class follows along. Choose students who can read loudly and clearly.

S1-1

3. After the story has been read, ask and discuss the following questions:

   a. How did Texter and Internetta get their names?

   Texter is a text-messaging expert and Internetta knows a lot about the Internet.

b. Texter says that Internetta is Internet savvy. Does anyone know what the word *savvy* means?

Explain that this is a new vocabulary word. Write it on the board and define it as "knowing a lot about something."

TEACHER TIP

Definition of bullying:
Bullying is when someone repeatedly and on purpose says or does mean or hurtful things to another person who has a hard time defending himself or herself.

c. The bus driver said that what Tony was doing to the new boy was bullying. Why did he think that?

The bus driver said that Tony was being mean on purpose to someone who was smaller or weaker than him, and he was doing it over and over.

d. What the bus driver said is really what bullying means. Does anyone remember what that is?

Bullying is picking on someone who has a hard time defending himself or herself by doing something mean or hurtful on purpose over and over again. In today's story, Tony trips the new boy, who is younger and smaller than him, every day. But people who bully don't always trip or touch the other person. Sometimes they call them names, tell lies about them, or decide not to include them in their group.

4. Ask the following questions (allow time for students to answer each question):

   a. Do you think Tony's friends were part of the bullying? Why or why not?

   b. What do you think about the other kids on the bus who saw what Tony was doing but didn't do anything?

   c. What do you think about what Texter and his friends did?

   d. What would you have done if you were on the bus?

Summarize these answers by saying:

Everyone who was on the bus was part of the bullying. They each played a different part. This is called the Bullying Circle.

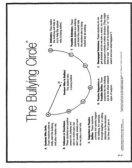

S1-2

5. Show The Bullying Circle diagram. Explain:

Tony's friends are followers and supporters. They cheered him on and laughed at the new boy. Some of them might have even joined in. The other students on the bus are the bystanders—they stand by and watch. Some might like the bullying but they don't show it. Some of them might not think anything good or bad about it. Others might not like the bullying but don't do anything about it. Some of the bystanders might stand up for and defend the person who is bullied. Think about what you said you would have done if you were on the bus. Think about the part you would have played.

6. Ask:

Without naming names, do you know of something like this happening in our school? What did you do? What did the other bystanders do?

Texter and Hector defended the new boy, but they also did something else to help him. What was it? *(They told an adult, the bus driver.)*

Summarize by saying:

If you are ever in a place where someone is being bullied, you can think about what part you want to play. How could you help the person who is bullied? Could you help them right now yourself? Could you get help? Could you tell an adult? These are all ways bystanders can take action.

S1-3

TEACHER TIP

If your class has already implemented the Olweus Bullying Prevention Program, *invite students to recite the rules and briefly explain what they mean.*

7. Show The Four Anti-Bullying Rules sheet. Explain:

Having rules to prevent bullying can help. Here are four rules to help stop bullying:

- **We will not bully others.** (Bullying is not acceptable.)

- **We will try to help students who are bullied.** (We can find an adult to help, and defend or befriend a student who is bullied.)

- **We will try to include students who are left out.** (Students who are bullied are often excluded.)

- **If we know that somebody is being bullied, we will tell an adult at school and an adult at home.** (Telling is not tattling or snitching, it is following the rules that there is no bullying allowed.)

8. Summarize by saying:

You are now savvy (remember our new word?) when it comes to bullying. Bullying is mean and hurtful. Now we're going to do something fun to help us remember the Four Anti-Bullying Rules.

PART 2
15 minutes

TEACHER TIP
Keep the rules up where students can see them as they prepare their raps.

▶ **Creating Rule Raps**

The purpose of part 2 is to help students remember and understand the rules to prevent bullying. They will create raps to explain the rules in a positive way.

1. Divide the class into pairs or groups of three. Explain to the class:

   Now we will make up some raps to go along with each rule. I will assign each pair (or group) a rule. Read over your rule and then write at least one two-line rap about it. Here are some examples:

   Rule: We will not bully others.

   Rap: Bullying is mean and bullying is cruel.
   We don't want bullying at our school.

   Rule: We will try to help students who are bullied.

   Rap: If someone bullies me or someone bullies you,
   We'll help each other out, that's what we should do!

2. Hand out paper and pencils to each group so they can write down their raps. Circulate around the room, helping groups as needed.

3. As time permits, invite students to recite their raps to the class.

   Here are some other options:

   • Option A: Have students take turns saying their raps every day over the P.A. system as part of the school announcements.

   • Option B: Have students create movements to go along with the raps and perform them for another class.

   • Option C: Videotape the students as they recite their raps.

PART 3
5 minutes

▶ **Conclusion and Homework Assignment**

1. Ask:

   What are some things that you can do if you are bullied or if you see someone else being bullied?

   Allow time for students to respond.

S1-4

2. Hand out Homework Assignment 1. Explain to the students:

   This is a homework lesson for you to do with a parent or an adult you live with. If the adult you live with is not able to do this assignment with you, then another adult could do it. This could be a relative, neighbor, or friend. If you have trouble finding an adult to do it with you, come and see me, and I will help you.

   You will have five of these homework assignments during the program. There are some activities for you to do with an adult. The activities you will do this week are

   - **Think about people who bully in movies, stories, or books. Your parent or other adult will also share a bullying experience that happened to them when they were growing up.**

   - **Talk about the Four Anti-Bullying Rules.**

   When you and the adult you work with have completed the homework, both of you need to sign the return slip at the end of the assignment. Then you will cut off the return slip and bring it back.

3. Show the students where to put their return slips.

4. Explain how students will be graded on this homework assignment.

5. Tell the students when the homework assignment will be due.

The definition of bullying, the "Bullying Circle," and the Four Anti-Bullying Rules are used with permission from Olweus, Dan, Susan P. Limber, Vicki Crocker Flerx, Nancy Mullin, Jane Riese, and Marlene Snyder. 2007. *Olweus bullying prevention program: Teacher guide.* Center City, MN: Hazelden Publishing.

What Is Cyber Bullying?

Description

Through a story, a large-group discussion, and a game, students will understand what cyber bullying is and recognize cyber bullying situations. They will also understand the importance of keeping their computer password, if they have one, a secret.

Student Learner Outcomes

By the end of this session, students will be able to

- define cyber bullying

- identify examples of cyber bullying

- understand the importance of not sharing passwords

Parent/Guardian Learner Outcomes

By reading the session 2 information and completing Homework Assignment 2 with their child, parents and guardians will be able to

- explain the definition of cyber bullying

- list the different technologies that their children will eventually be using

- describe how to show their child how important it is that only they and their child know their child's password (Internet safety)

SESSION 2 AT A GLANCE

Total Time: 40 minutes

Part 1:
Story and Discussion
(15 minutes)

Part 2:
Definition of Cyber Bullying
(5 minutes)

Part 3:
Know It Show It Game
(15 minutes)

Part 4:
Conclusion and Homework Assignment
(5 minutes)

• explain how prevalent and serious cyber bullying can become

Materials Needed

☐ CD-ROM materials

• Session 2: The Story  S2-1

• Cyber Bullying HURTS poster I-14

• Know It Show It Situations S2-2

• Know It Show It Game Sheet S2-3

• Know It Show It Game Answer Sheet S2-4

• Homework Assignment 2 S2-5 (SP)

☐ pencils

Preparation Needed

1. Print out and copy the Session 2: The Story handout, one per student.

2. Print out the poster. Enlarge and hang it up in your classroom where students can see it.

3. Print out and copy the Know It Show It Game Sheet, one per student team.

4. Print out and copy Homework Assignment 2, one per student.

S E S S I O N   ② O U T L I N E

PART 1
15 minutes

▶ **Story and Discussion**

The purpose of part 1 is to read and discuss the second story, which will help students understand what cyber bullying is and why it is important to keep computer passwords a secret. Students will also learn the HURT acronym to help them remember what cyber bullying is and how it affects others.

1. Explain to the students:

   Today we are going to read another story about Texter and Internetta. In the last story they helped a boy who was bullied. How would you explain what bullying is to someone who didn't know?

   Answers should include these points:

   a. Doing something mean or hurtful on purpose.

   b. Doing these mean things over and over.

   c. Picking on someone who has a hard time defending himself or herself.

   As you listen to this story, think about how you would answer this question: What is cyber bullying?

S2-1

2. Hand out the story for session 2 to each student. Read the story aloud or call on students to read the story aloud while the class follows along.

3. Ask and discuss the following questions:

   a. **Why did Tracy need Netta's help?**

      Someone was sending messages to boys that seemed as if they were from her.

b. How was Jessica able to send messages that seemed as if they were from Tracy?

She was using Tracy's password.

c. Why is it important to keep your password a secret?

If you share your password with someone, that person could send messages that look as if they are from you.

d. Netta explained what cyber bullying is. What is it?

Cyber bullying is when someone bullies you through computers or cell phones.

e. Have you ever heard of anything like this happening at school or to someone you know? Please explain without using names.

PART 2
5 minutes

CYBER BULLYING HURTS

Harmful on purpose
Uses power
Repeated
Technology carries the message

I-14

▶ **Definition of Cyber Bullying**

1. Show the Cyber Bullying HURTS poster. Explain:

   Here is one way to remember what cyber bullying is. It is important to know what it is and that it hurts other people.

2. Go through the poster with the class. Emphasize the following points:

   a. Harmful on purpose. In the story, Jessica said what she did was just a joke. Cyber bullying is not a joke. It is done on purpose, and it is meant to hurt someone.

   b. Uses power. People who bully or cyber bully often pick on someone who seems weaker or not as popular. They usually choose people who can't easily defend themselves. People who cyber bully feel as though they are more powerful than the people they pick on. And they don't think that anyone will know who they are.

c. **Repeated.** Just like bullying, cyber bullying happens over and over. This can be by sending messages over and over again. It can also be by sending one message to many people or posting something on a Web page that many people will see. It is possible for hundreds of people to see a message or photo in just a few minutes.

d. **Technology carries the message.** Cyber bullying happens through cell phones and text messages (sending written messages to other cell phones), emails (sending electronic mail), instant messaging (having a live, written conversation online), chat rooms (places where you can have a live, written conversation with more than one person), Web pages, and social-networking sites (places to connect with friends online).

3. Summarize by saying:

Now you know what cyber bullying is. You know that it is mean and hurts people. Sometimes people *send* messages they would never *say* to someone's face. They wouldn't say it because it is mean or because they would not want anyone to know they said it. You might not use cell phones or instant messaging right now, but it's good to know about this for the future.

PART 3
15 minutes

▶ **Know It Show It Game**

The purpose of part 3 is for students to identify cyber bullying situations and understand why these situations could be considered cyber bullying.

TEACHER TIP
Review the Know It Show It Situations ahead of time to make sure they are appropriate for your classroom. If there have been incidents of cyber bullying in your class or your school, you might want to add similar situations to the game, but be careful to keep these situations anonymous.

1. Explain to the students:

   Now we are going to play the Know It Show It Game. You know what cyber bullying is. Now you will show what you know. You will be working in teams for this game.

2. Divide the class into teams of three to four students. Give each team the Know It Show It Game Sheet and pencils.

3. Explain:

   I'll read a situation. Then we will figure out how it fits into each part of the definition of cyber bullying. After we do this first example, you will work with your team on the next situations.

S2-3

4. Read aloud the first situation for the Know It Show It Situations. Make sure that students can still see the Cyber Bullying HURTS poster.

5. Read the first situation aloud:

   Tasha was new to her school. She was just starting to make friends. A popular girl in the class thought Tasha was going to take away her friends. She started sending Tasha mean text messages every day saying that nobody liked her.

S2-2

6. Using the poster, go through each letter in H-U-R-T and call on students to explain how what happened to Tasha was cyber bullying. As students give their answers, fill in a game sheet so they can see how to do it. For example:

   H—She tried to make Tasha feel bad.

   U—She was popular so that gave her some power over Tasha.

   R—The messages were sent every day.

   T—The messages were text messages sent by cell phone.

   Refer to the Know It Show It Game Answer Sheet if necessary.

S2-4

7. Explain to the students:

   Now I will read the next situation. Choose one person in your group to write on the game sheet. With your team you will decide how it fits into each part of the cyber bullying definition. Once you have each part filled in, your team should stand up. The first team to stand will win a point if they are correct. If they are not correct, the second team to stand will have a chance to answer.

8. Read the next situation. Allow students time to fill in their game sheets. Call on the first group that stood up to read their answers. If they are correct, give them one point. If they are not correct, ask the second team that stood up to give their answers. Read as many situations as time permits. The group with the most points is cyber bullying savvy.

PART 4
5 minutes

▶ **Conclusion and Homework Assignment**

1. Ask the students:

   What are some ways that people can be cyber bullied?

   Text messaging, IMing, email, Web sites, social-networking sites, etc.

   Now you know what cyber bullying is. Even if you don't have a cell phone or use a computer, you might use someone else's. You might hear about something like this happening. Make sure you tell an adult if you do.

2. Hand out Homework Assignment 2. Explain to the students:

   This homework assignment is for you to do with your parent or an adult that you live with. If it is not possible for an adult you live with to do it with you, then another adult like a relative or neighbor could. If you have trouble finding an adult to work with, come and see me, and I will help you.

   This is the second homework assignment of the program. There are some activities for you to do with an adult. The activities this week are

   - **checking out safe Web sites for kids**

   - **taking a true/false quiz about cyber bullying**

   When you and the adult you work with have completed the homework, both of you need to sign the return slip at the bottom of the sheet. Then you will cut off the return slip and bring it back.

3. Show the students where to put their return slips.

S2-5

4. Explain how students will be graded on this homework assignment.

5. Tell the students when the homework assignment will be due.

Keep your password a secret!

If you share your password with someone, that person could send messages that look as if they are from you.

How Does Cyber Bullying Affect People?

Description

Through a story and a large-group discussion, students will understand how cyber bullying affects the student who is bullied, the student who bullies others, and bystanders. Through an active game, students will have an opportunity to react empathetically to a variety of situations.

Student Learner Outcomes

By the end of this session, students will be able to

- identify the effects of cyber bullying

- empathize with people who are cyber bullied

Parent/Guardian Learner Outcomes

By reading the session 3 information and completing Homework Assignment 3 with their child, parents and guardians will be able to

- know that though most cyber bullying happens outside school, it does have ramifications in school

- explain the social and emotional harm cyber bullying can inflict

- describe what some of the academic consequences of cyber bullying can be

- know that they have control over their children's online activities

**SESSION 3
AT A GLANCE**

Total Time: 40 minutes

Part 1:
Story and Discussion
(20 minutes)

Part 2:
Technology Ups
and Downs
(15 minutes)

Part 3:
Conclusion
and Homework
Assignment
(5 minutes)

Materials Needed

☐ CD-ROM materials

- Session 3: The Story S3-1

- Technology Ups and Downs Activity Situations S3-2

- Homework Assignment 3 S3-3 (SP)

- Cyber Bullying HURTS poster (used in session 2)

Preparation Needed

1. Print out and copy the Session 3: The Story handout, one per student.

2. Print out the Technology Ups and Downs Activity Situations.

3. Print out and copy Homework Assignment 3, one per student.

4. Hang the Cyber Bullying HURTS poster in a place where students can see it.

PART 1
20 minutes

▶ **Story and Discussion**

The purpose of part 1 is to read and discuss the third story, which will help students understand the effects of cyber bullying.

1. Explain to the students:

   Today we are going to read another story about Texter and Internetta. In the last story, Jessica used Tracy's password to send messages to boys in her class. This is one kind of cyber bullying. What is cyber bullying?

   Cyber bullying is when someone bullies you through computers or cell phones.

2. Refer to the Cyber Bullying HURTS poster. Review the HURT acronym by calling on students to read each part of the acronym.

S3-1

3. Explain to the students:

   As you listen to this story, think about how you would answer this question: What happens to the people in the story because of cyber bullying?

   Hand out the story for session 3 to each student. Read the story aloud or call on students to read the story aloud while the class follows along.

4. Ask and discuss the following questions:

   a. How was Charlie being cyber bullied?

   Someone was sending him mean text messages.

b. Who was sending the messages to Charlie?

Matt.

c. What was Eric's part in the bullying?

He was a bystander. He knew about the bullying but didn't do anything about it.

d. What does it mean to be a bystander?

Being a bystander means you are not the person who is bullied or the person who is doing the bullying. A bystander sees the bullying and knows it is going on. In the case of cyber bullying, a bystander could be someone who reads a message or sees a photo that is part of the bullying.

e. Why would Matt say that sending the messages was just a joke?

Maybe he thought he wouldn't get in trouble if he said he didn't mean it.

f. What happened to each of the kids in the story because of the cyber bullying?

- Charlie—He felt sad and upset, didn't act like himself, didn't want to come to school, worried that mean tricks were going to be played on him or that he would get hurt, didn't do his schoolwork (science project), and was afraid to look at his text messages.

- Eric—He got in a bit of trouble because he could have done something to stop the cyber bullying but didn't, and he was taken advantage of by Matt, who used his cell phone.

- Matt—He got in trouble.

- Texter—He was mad at Charlie, had to do a lot of the work on the science project by himself, did the right thing to help Charlie out, and did the right thing by telling Charlie to tell his parents.

g. How would you have felt if you were Charlie?

5. Summarize student responses by including these points:

Students who are cyber bullied by someone may

- **feel sad, upset, scared, nervous, worried, sad**

- **feel like they don't want to go to school**

- **not like themselves very much**

- **sometimes lose friends because of the bullying**

What would you have done if you were Eric and your friend wanted to use your phone to cyber bully someone?

Add to the discussion by including these points:

A bystander's job is to do something about the bullying. This could be

- **telling an adult**

- **trying to stop the person doing the bullying without bullying back (if they feel safe doing this)**

- **not helping the person doing the bullying, as Eric did**

- **not encouraging the person doing the bullying by laughing, telling them to do it, joining in, etc.**

6. Summarize by saying:

Cyber bullying can be hurtful in many ways. People who do the cyber bullying can get in a lot of trouble. The people who are cyber bullied feel sad, scared, and upset. If you are a bystander, remember:

Don't *stand by* and watch it happen; *stand up* for people being bullied and help them out. *Always* tell an adult.

PART 2
15 minutes

▶ **Technology Ups and Downs**

The purpose of part 2 is for students to think about how it would feel to be cyber bullied and how they could use technology in a positive way.

1. Have all the students stand up. Explain to the students:

   Now we're going to do an activity that will make you think about how it would feel to have different kinds of messages sent to you or about you. The messages might be on the computer or a cell phone. I'll read a situation. If that situation would hurt your feelings or make you feel bad, squat down. If it would make you feel happy, jump up. If it wouldn't make you feel happy or sad, then just keep standing. Everyone should return to standing to hear the next situation.

S3-2

2. Read one situation from the Technology Ups and Downs Activity Situations sheet as an example. Remind the students to squat, stand, or jump. After they react, they should all stand to hear the next situation. Continue by reading the situations and giving the students a chance to react to them.

PART 3
5 minutes

▶ **Conclusion and Homework Assignment**

1. Summarize the session by saying:

   Cell phones and computers can be used in many ways. Sometimes the way people use them makes us feel good. Sometimes we use them just to talk with each other. Sometimes they are used to hurt and embarrass people. If you have used cell phones or computers, think about how you would feel if you received the messages you are sending. You can't see the person who gets the message. But you need to remember that there is a real person on the other side of the screen.

It's also important to remember what to do if you are a bystander. Don't just stand by, stand up!

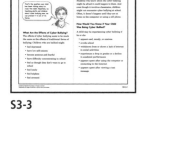

S3-3

2. Hand out Homework Assignment 3. Explain to the students:

This homework assignment is for you to do with your parent or an adult that you live with. If it is not possible for an adult you live with to do it with you, then another adult like a relative or neighbor could. If you have trouble finding an adult to work with, come and see me, and I will help you.

This is the third homework assignment of the program. There are some activities for you to do with an adult. The activities this week are

- talking more about the story the adult told you in the first homework lesson

- talking about how cyber bulling can hurt as much or more than other kinds of bullying

When you and the adult you work with have completed the homework, both of you need to sign the return slip on the last page. Then you will cut off the return slip and bring it back.

3. Show the students where to put their return slips.

4. Explain how students will be graded on this homework assignment.

5. Tell the students when the homework assignment will be due.

How Do I Treat People Well When I Use Technology?

Description

Through a story, a large-group discussion, and the creation of posters, students will learn the basic rules of netiquette.

Student Learner Outcomes

By the end of this session, students will be able to

- define what *netiquette* is

- identify basic rules of netiquette for online communication

Parent/Guardian Learner Outcomes

By reading the session 4 information and completing Homework Assignment 4 with their child, parents and guardians will be able to

- know basic online courtesy, or netiquette

- know how important family rules are regarding the use of the Internet, cell phones, cameras, and instant messaging

Materials Needed

- ☐ CD-ROM materials

  - Session 4: The Story ▯ S4-1

  - Netta-Kit poster ▯ I-15

**SESSION 4
AT A GLANCE**

Total Time: 40 minutes

Part 1:
Story and Discussion
(15 minutes)

Part 2:
Make a Message
(20 minutes)

Part 3:
Conclusion
and Homework
Assignment
(5 minutes)

• Homework Assignment 4 ⬜ S4-2 (SP)

☐ pencils

☐ construction paper

☐ crayons or markers

Preparation Needed

1. Print out and copy the Session 4: The Story handout, one per student.

2. Print out, enlarge, and hang the Netta-Kit poster.

3. Print out and copy Homework Assignment 4, one per student.

SESSION 4 OUTLINE

PART 1
15 minutes

▶ **Story and Discussion**

The purpose of part 1 is to read and discuss the fourth story, which will help students understand basic rules of netiquette for children and teens.

1. Explain to the students:

   Today we are going to read another story about Texter and Internetta. In the last story, Charlie was cyber bullied by Matt. Matt used Eric's cell phone to send mean text messages to Charlie. How does cyber bullying make people feel?

   Possible answers include sad, anxious, not wanting to go to school, fearful.

2. Ask:

   What does "Don't stand by, stand up!" mean?

   Answer: Don't *stand by* and watch cyber bullying happen; *stand up* for people being bullied and help them out.

3. Explain to the students:

   As you listen to today's story, think about how you would answer this question: What are some things to think about when you are using a computer or phone to send a message?

4. Hand out the story for session 4 to each student. Read the story aloud or call on students to read the story aloud while the class follows along.

S4-1

5. Ask and discuss the following questions:

   a. Why did Texter say that Sam Sandello was the problem?

   He was taking embarrassing pictures of kids with his cell phone camera and passing them around.

   b. How would you feel if Sam did that to you?

   c. Why were Ming and Abby arguing on IM?

   Abby said that she would never want to go to a movie with Ming. She said she was only kidding, but Ming couldn't tell that from the message.

   d. Why didn't Ming know that Abby was kidding?

   • Ming couldn't see Abby's expression or hear her tone of voice because they were online, so she couldn't tell that Abby was kidding.

   • Abby didn't say she was kidding in the message.

6. Ask:

   Have you ever heard of the word *netiquette*? Do you know what it means?

   Write the words *Internet* and *etiquette* on the board. After you explain how the word was made, write *netiquette* below them.

   ***Netiquette* is a new word that was made by combining the words *Internet* and *etiquette*. Etiquette is rules about how to behave, like saying "please" and "thank you" or putting your napkin on your lap. It's kind of like manners. What do you think *netiquette* means?**

   Netiquette is like having good manners when you are using technology. It's about being respectful when you send messages through the computer or cell phone. That's really

what the song in the story was about. Take a look at the song. What are some netiquette rules in the song?

7. Show the Netta-Kit poster and explain:

Netta decided to put the netiquette ideas into a kit for other kids. She called it a Netta-Kit.

8. Read or call on students to read each item on the poster. Here is the poster text:

When You're on the Net or on a Phone, Don't Forget Your Netta-Kit!

- **Only talk to people that you really know (not friends of friends).**

- **Don't send or post anything online that you wouldn't say in person.**

- **Don't send anything you wouldn't want to receive yourself.**

- **Remember, there is a real person receiving your message.**

- **Make sure your messages say what you mean. You might have to explain yourself.**

- **Use an emoticon to show how you're feeling. Examples: :-) is happy; :-(is sad.**

- **Don't send a message when you are angry. Wait until you cool down.**

- **Don't send private or embarrassing information about you or anyone else to others.**

- **Don't use all capital letters—it's like yelling online.**

- **Ask permission before taking or sending a photo of someone online or through your cell phone.**

I-15

Duplicating this page is illegal. Do not copy this material without written permission from the publisher.

75

9. Summarize by saying:

You will get a copy of the Netta-Kit in your homework assignment this week. Cut it out and put it near your computer at home, if you have one. You might not be using a computer or cell phone to talk to your friends just yet, but you may use them when you are older. When you do, you will already know about netiquette. If you are using a computer or cell phone now, these are important rules to remember and follow.

PART 2
20 minutes

TEACHER TIP
This activity could be done in groups of three, four, or five students.

▶ **Make a Message**

The purpose of part 2 is for students to explain the Netta-Kit rules to each other by creating posters.

1. Explain to the students:

Now that you know the Netta-Kit rules, it's time to let everyone else know about them. One way to get information out to a lot of people at once is through posters. Today you will work in small groups to create a poster about one of the Netta-Kit rules.

2. Divide the class into ten small groups. If you have more than ten small groups, two groups can work on the same rule. If you have fewer than ten small groups, some groups can work on two rules and combine them into one poster, if possible.

3. Assign each small group one rule to work on.

4. Explain:

As you create them, remember that these posters should show or explain the rule so kids will

- **know the rule**

- **understand what it means**

- **know why it is important**

5. Circulate among the small groups while they are working to answer any questions they might have.

6. When they are ready, call on each small group to show and explain their poster. Then hang them in order around your classroom.

PART 3
5 minutes

S4-2

▶ **Conclusion and Homework Assignment**

1. Explain:

   You now know a lot about netiquette. Be sure to think about the Netta-Kit rules when you use the computer or a cell phone, and remember to be polite to others even if they can't see or hear you.

2. Hand out Homework Assignment 4. Explain to the students:

   This homework assignment is for you to do with your parent or an adult that you live with. If it is not possible for an adult you live with to do it with you, then another adult like a relative or neighbor could. If you have trouble finding an adult to work with, come and see me, and I will help you.

   This is the fourth homework assignment of the program. There are some activities for you to do with an adult. The activities this week are

   - **creating family rules about using the Internet, computers, or cell phones**

   - **making a list of all the great ways to use the Internet**

When you and the adult you work with have completed the homework, both of you need to sign the return slip on the last page. Then you will cut off the return slip and bring it back.

3. Show the students where to put their return slips.

4. Explain how students will be graded on this homework assignment.

5. Tell the students when the homework assignment will be due.

CYBER BULLYING   SESSION 5

What Do I Do if Someone Is Mean to Me through Technology?

Description

Through a story, a large-group discussion, and a class game, students will learn what they can do if they or someone they know is cyber bullied.

Student Learner Outcomes

By the end of this session, students will be able to

- identify possible responses to cyber bullying situations

- know that part of being safe online means telling an adult if they experience cyber bullying

- know that telling an adult when they or someone they know is being cyber bullied is not "tattling"

Parent/Guardian Learner Outcomes

By reading the session 5 information and completing Homework Assignment 5 with their child, parents and guardians will be able to

- explain what their options are if their child is cyber bullied

- describe what they can do if their child's friend is cyber bullied

- explain how cyber bullying others and being cyber bullied can affect their child's online reputation

SESSION 5 AT A GLANCE

Total Time: 40 minutes

Part 1:
Story and Discussion
(20 minutes)

Part 2:
Who Got the Message?
(15 minutes)

Part 3:
Conclusion and Homework Assignment
(5 minutes)

• describe how research shows that children don't tell about cyber bullying for fear of losing cell phone and Internet privileges; *know not to make that a consequence*

Materials Needed

☐ CD-ROM materials

- Session 5: The Story ▢ S5-1
- TELL KIDS TELL handout ▢ S5-2
- Who Got the Message? Game Squares ▢ S5-3
- Who Got the Message? Messages ▢ S5-4
- Homework Assignment 5 ▢ S5-5 (SP)

☐ overhead projector or LCD projector

☐ Netta-Kit poster (used in session 4)

☐ pencils

☐ CD player or some music source that can be turned on and off

☐ optional: transparency sheets

Preparation Needed

1. Print out and copy the Session 5: The Story handout, one per student.

2. If using an overhead projector, print out and copy TELL KIDS TELL onto transparency sheets. If using an LCD projector, have the CD-ROM document ready to show.

3. Print out, copy, and cut out the Who Got the Message? Game Squares, one square per student.

4. Print out one copy of the Who Got the Message? Messages.

5. Cue the music on the CD player and have that ready to go.

6. Print out and copy Homework Assignment 5, one per student.

7. Hang the Netta-Kit poster where students can see it.

S E S S I O N **5** O U T L I N E

PART 1
20 minutes

▶ **Story and Discussion**

The purpose of part 1 is to read and discuss the fifth story, which will help students learn how to respond to cyber bullying if it happens to them or someone they know.

1. Explain to the students:

   Today we are going to read another story about Texter and Internetta. In the last story we read, Texter, Internetta, and some of their friends started a band. They came up with a song about netiquette. What does *netiquette* mean?

   Answer: It means being respectful of others and having good manners online.

I-15

2. Refer to the Netta-Kit poster. Ask:

   Netta created a Netta-Kit with these rules. Read aloud each rule. **Which ones do you think are the most important? Why?** Allow time for several students to answer.

3. Explain to the students:

   As you listen to today's story, think about how you would answer this question: What could you do if you or someone you know is being cyber bullied?

S5-1

4. Hand out the story for session 5 to each student. Read the story aloud or call on students to read the story aloud while the class follows along.

5. Discuss the following questions:

   a. Why did Alicia think that Elena was allergic to computers?

   She got in a bad mood when she used the computer and sometimes started crying.

   b. What was really happening to Elena?

   Some girls were cyber bullying her on IM and MySpace.

   c. What was Elena's first reaction to the cyber bullying?

   She ignored it.

   d. Why did Netta think that Elena should save the cyber bullying messages?

   Elena might need to prove that the girls were cyber bullying and would need a copy of the messages to do it.

   e. Why is it important to tell an adult if you or someone you know is being cyber bullied?

   • An adult might be able to help stop the cyber bullying.

   • An adult could call another child's parents or the school.

6. Explain to the students:

   If you or someone you know is being cyber bullied, there are things that you could do. You learned about some of them in the story. Here is one way to think about what you should do.

S5-2

7. Show the TELL KIDS TELL handout using the transparency or the LCD. Go through each item with the class making the following points:

   TELL—If you or someone you know gets a mean message through the computer or cell phone, you should tell your parents and another adult, like your teacher, right away. If you know that someone else is getting mean messages, you should also tell an adult right away.

An adult will help you go through the next steps.

***Kick* them off your friends list**—If you get mean messages through IM (or a social-networking site like MySpace), you should have your parents or another adult help you take that person off your friends or buddy list. If you do that, then they won't be able to send you the messages. This might stop the person from sending any more messages.

***Ignore* the message**—If you get one mean message, you could just try ignoring it. People who send mean messages want to make you angry or hurt your feelings. If they think your feelings aren't hurt, they might stop. If you keep getting messages like this, then you should tell an adult.

***Don't* respond**—Don't answer the message. If you are angry and answer back, then you might say mean things. Remember, the person sending the message wants you to get angry. Bullying is harmful on purpose. Even if you feel angry, don't let senders know that their plan worked.

***Save* the evidence**—Save the messages. You might need to prove that you got them. Have your parents or another adult help you print the messages or save them to the desktop. Do not delete these messages.

***TELL* an adult**—If you or someone you know keeps getting mean messages, or someone keeps sending messages about you, tell an adult right away, like your parents and your teacher. Telling an adult isn't tattling. Telling an adult is standing up for yourself or someone you know. No one should be able to cyber bully someone else. Sometimes telling an adult takes courage. *Courage* is an important word for this week.

8. Summarize by saying:

   Remember to TELL KIDS TELL if you or someone you know is being cyber bullied.

PART 2
15 minutes

S5-3

▶ **Who Got the Message? Game**

The purpose of part 2 is for students to practice responding to a variety of online and text messages.

Note: You will need one game square with a cell phone on it, one with a computer on it, and the rest blank. There should be one square per student, including these two. Before giving the squares to the students, fold them in half so they cannot see whether they have a blank square or not. You will also need a CD player or some other music source that you can turn on and off.

If there have been instances of cyber bullying at your school, you might want to include similar situations in the game messages, but be sure not to use the names of those involved.

1. Invite students to sit in a circle. Explain:

   We are now going to play a game called "Who Got the Message?" I am going to give each of you a folded square of paper. Don't open it. When I play the music you will pass the paper to the person sitting to your left and the person to your right will pass a paper to you.

   You should only have one paper at a time. You will be passing with your left hand and receiving with your right hand. When the music stops, you can open the folded square that you have in your right hand. Everyone should have one folded square. If you have a square that has a cell phone on it, I will ask you what you would do if you got a certain text message. If you have a folded square that has a computer on it, I will ask you what you would do if you got a certain message on the computer. If your square is blank, you won't be answering a question.

2. Hand out one folded square to each student.

3. Play the game as follows:

- Begin playing the music and directing the movement of the game squares.

- Turn off the music and make sure that each student has one game square. (Play the music for no longer than 20 seconds.)

- Tell students to open the squares.

- Ask who has the cell phone.

- Read a text message from Who Got the Message? Messages.

- Ask the student who has the cell phone square how he or she would feel and what he or she would do if he or she received this message.

- Ask who has the computer.

- Read a computer message from Who Got the Message? Messages.

- Ask the student who has the computer square how he or she would feel and what he or she would do if he or she received this message.

- Discuss both student's answers.

- Tell the students to fold their squares again.

- Turn on the music and tell the students to pass the squares again.

- Continue playing as time permits.

S5-4

Cyber Bullying Hurts

PART 3
5 minutes

▶ **Conclusion and Homework Assignment**

1. Discuss the following questions:

   • **What should you do if your friend is getting mean messages on his or her cell phone?**

   Tell your parents and teacher, save the messages, and show the messages to the adults you told.

   • **What should you do if you are getting mean messages when you're on IM on your family's computer?**

   Tell your parents and teacher, save the messages, remove the person who is sending the messages from your friends or buddy list, and show the messages to the adults you told.

2. Review the TELL KIDS TELL handout with the students.

S5-5

3. Hand out Homework Assignment 5. Explain to the students:

   This homework assignment is for you to do with your parent or an adult that you live with. If it is not possible for an adult you live with to do it with you, then another adult like a relative or neighbor could. If you have trouble finding an adult to work with, come and see me, and I will help you.

   This is the fifth homework assignment of the program. There are some activities for you to do with an adult. The activities this week are:

   • **role-playing what you and the adult you are working with would do if you were cyber bullied**

   • **filling out a contract with the adult you are working with about what each of you will do if you are ever cyber bullied**

When you and the adult you are working with have completed the homework assignment, both of you need to sign the return slip on the last page. Then you will cut off the return slip and bring it back.

4. Show the students where to put their return slips.

5. Explain how students will be graded on this homework assignment.

6. Tell the students when the homework assignment will be due.

Extend the Learning Suggestions

You may wish to have students do small-group or individual projects to enhance and reinforce learning. These projects might involve teaching others in their class, at school, or in the community about cyber bullying. When students teach others, they are forced to demonstrate a clear understanding of the concepts. Teaching others will help students see themselves as role models for other students. You might want to have students work on a variety of projects and invite parents or other school staff to see them. Here are some suggestions for projects and assignments:

- create a cyber bullying prevention Web page
- create a Web page to report bullying
- teach younger students in the school about cyber bullying prevention and Internet safety
- have a poster campaign or contest
- write an article for the school newsletter
- write a story about cyber bullying
- act out the Texter and Internetta stories
- create a Texter and Internetta comic
- take a poll about cyber bullying in your class or in your school
- make posters for the local library
- find stories about cyber bullying in newspapers
- create a cyber club for students who need help

Additional Materials

Teacher Training Preparation

Description

This outline includes directions for conducting a three-hour training for facilitators/teachers of *Cyber Bullying: A Prevention Curriculum for Grades 3–5*. Adapt this outline to fit the needs and time frame of your group.

Who Should Conduct the Training?

Ideally, several staff and faculty members at the school who help to coordinate the school's bullying prevention activities will conduct the training. For schools that are implementing the *Olweus Bullying Prevention Program (OBPP),* this training would be led by individuals on the Bullying Prevention Coordinating Committee. If such a committee does not already exist, you may find it beneficial to form one. Members should include an administrator; a teacher from each grade; a school counselor, school psychologist, or other school-based mental health professional; a representative of the nonteaching staff; one or two parents; and other school personnel (e.g., a nurse, school resource officer, Title IX representative) as appropriate.

Materials Needed

- ☐ copies of the *Cyber Bullying: A Prevention Curriculum for Grades 3–5* curriculum (one per person)

- ☐ name tags

- ☐ marker

☐ pens or pencils

☐ masking tape

☐ one piece of poster board

☐ construction paper

☐ crayons or markers

☐ your school's policy(ies) on bullying and cyber bullying (if available), as well as the acceptable use of technology policy

☐ located on the CD-ROM:

- Glossary of Cyber Terms 🖨 I-11 (SP) *(also on pages 33–36 of this manual)*
- Internet Safety Tips for Parents and Guardians 🖨 I-12 (SP) *(also on pages 37–40 of this manual)*
- The Bullying Circle diagram 🖨 S1-2
- Cyber Bullying HURTS poster 🖨 I-14
- Know It Show It Game situations, game sheet, and answer sheet 🖨 S2-2, S2-3, S2-4
- stories for sessions 1–5 🖨 S1-1, S2-1, S3-1, S4-1, S5-1
- Homework Assignment 3 🖨 S3-3 (SP)
- TELL KIDS TELL handout 🖨 S5-2
- *Optional:* computer and LCD projector (for additional background information on cyber bullying included as a Teacher Training presentation on the CD-ROM)
- *Optional:* refreshments (highly recommended)

Preparation Needed

1. Select a training room where participants will be comfortable sitting and interacting for three hours. Arrange the chairs in a circle or at small tables, so people will be more open to discussing this sensitive topic with others. Also make sure the room temperature is comfortable.

2. *Optional:* Set up refreshments.

3. Read through this training outline and the curriculum, so you are comfortable teaching others.

4. Write the Four Anti-Bullying Rules (session 1, page 48) on the sheet of poster board.

5. Print out and copy The Bullying Circle diagram, one per participant.

6. Print out and enlarge both the Cyber Bullying HURTS poster and the Netta-Kit poster, and hang them in a place where all participants can see them.

7. Photocopy the Know It Show It situations, game sheet (one per group), and answer sheet.

8. Highlight statistics from surveys of your own students (e.g., from the Olweus Bullying Questionnaire) regarding bullying and cyber bullying. If these statistics are not available, research local or state statistics on bullying and/or cyber bullying, or use the statistics provided on the CD-ROM.

   Optional: Cofacilitate this training with someone who has a strong background in these statistics.

9. Photocopy all other CD-ROM content (one set per person).

Teacher Training Outline

Introduction (30 minutes)

1. Welcome participants and give each person a name tag (if they may not all know each other).

2. Introduce yourself and your cotrainer(s) and briefly state why you have chosen to train others in the use of *Cyber Bullying: A Prevention Curriculum for Grades 3–5.*

3. Have people introduce themselves and share briefly why they are interested in teaching this cyber bullying curriculum.

4. Briefly describe the main content of the cyber bullying curriculum, paraphrasing the wording in the introduction (pages 1–3).

5. Briefly describe the main components of the curriculum, including the five sessions, which include the Internetta and Texter stories, the games and activities, and the parent/guardian newsletters (see curriculum introduction). Hand out copies of the *Cyber Bullying* curriculum, if desired.

6. Highlight and discuss the introductory pages that describe what teachers should be aware of and other guidelines as they teach the curriculum (pages 6–8).

S1-3

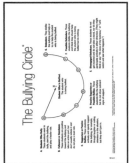

S1-2

Defining Bullying (10 minutes)

1. As a group, discuss or review the definition of *bullying* (see page 46 in session 1).

2. Display and discuss the Four Anti-Bullying Rules from the *Olweus Bullying Prevention Program.* If your school is not already following these rules, discuss how they can be implemented in elementary school classrooms. If your school has already adopted these rules as part of *OBPP,* discuss how they relate to cyber bullying (on and off campus).

3. Distribute and discuss The Bullying Circle diagram and the roles that people play in bullying situations.

4. Briefly share school-level, local, or national statistics on bullying and cyber bullying. Try to personalize this information as much as possible, so participants more clearly see the importance of addressing this issue with their students.

Defining Cyber Bullying (30 minutes)

CYBER BULLYING HURTS

Harmful on purpose
Uses power
Repeated
Technology carries the message

I-14

S2-3

1. Divide participants into groups of three or four people. Have them brainstorm a list of ways they know of that people can cyber bully.

2. Have each group briefly share a few ideas from their lists. Add to the discussion, as necessary.

3. Show and discuss the Cyber Bullying HURTS poster, using the format from session 2, part 2, the "Definition of Cyber Bullying" on page 56–57 of this curriculum.

4. Keep participants in their small groups. Hand out one Know It Show It Game Sheet and pencils to each group. Play the game as it is described in session 2, part 3, starting on page 58 of the curriculum. This will give participants a sense of how children will play the game to help them understand what cyber bullying is.

5. Hand out the Glossary of Cyber Terms and Internet Safety Tips for Parents and Guardians and briefly go through them.

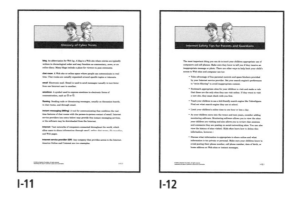

I-11   I-12

The Effects of Cyber Bullying (30 minutes)

1. Share what the warning signs or "red flags" are that someone may be cyber bullying others or being cyber bullied (see the introduction, page 12). Stress the importance of teachers being aware of these warning signs, being proactive in talking with these students to determine what is wrong, and taking action when necessary.

I-13

2. *Optional:* Review some of the data from the CD-ROM Teacher Training Presentation on possible effects of cyber bullying on students.

3. Hand out the Texter and Internetta stories. Briefly describe each character.

4. Have participants turn to the story for session 3.

S3-1

5. Invite a participant to read the story aloud. Starting with step 4 of part 1 on page 65, discuss the story as described through the end of part 1. This will give participants an idea of how these stories will be used in each session.

6. Hand out Homework Assignment 3 so that participants can read through the information parents and guardians receive and see how parents/guardians and students can work together to complete the assignment, thus achieving the Student and Parent/Guardian Learner Outcomes.

Break (10 minutes)

1. *Optional:* Provide refreshments.

S3-3

I-15

Netiquette (30 minutes)

1. Ask if anyone knows what the word *netiquette* means. Give the definition and background information found in session 4, part 1, page 74.

2. Show the Netta-Kit poster and describe how it is used in the session.

3. Hand out the construction paper and crayons or markers. Starting with session 4, part 2, page 76, do the Make a Message activity with the group.

4. When they are ready, call on each small group to show and explain their poster.

   If available, read and discuss your school's policy on cyber bullying. If your school has a policy on bullying that does not specifically mention cyber bullying, discuss how the policy may relate to cyber bullying on (or off) campus. (See the CD-ROM for more information about development of policies on cyber bullying.) I-2, I-3, I-7 If you do not have a cyber bullying policy, you may have an acceptable use of technology policy that mentions cyber bullying or other inappropriate uses of campus technology.

I-2

I-3

I-7

What Can Students Do if Someone Is Mean to Them through Technology? (20 minutes)

S5-2

1. Distribute the TELL KIDS TELL handout.

2. Discuss the handout and how teachers and other school staff can help students feel more comfortable reporting incidents of cyber bullying.

3. Take time to discuss your school's reporting policy of cyber bullying incidents for teachers and other school staff. Be sure to talk about situations when the police should be involved (for example, if the cyber bullying is racially motivated, if it includes threats to harm, if it is defamatory in nature, etc.)

Concluding Activities (20 minutes)

1. If you have a group of school educators, be sure to share with them the Scope and Sequence and Related National Academic Standards information in the curriculum introduction.

2. Take time to answer any questions participants may have. Also spend time discussing any special adaptations that may be needed for their specific situations.

3. Finish up by having participants discuss and write down several goals for using *Cyber Bullying: A Prevention Curriculum for Grades 3–5*. On a piece of paper, have participants write their basic plan (e.g., When will implementation begin? How often will the curriculum be taught? During what class(es)? How will efforts be evaluated?). It is important that participants have concrete plans for implementation when they leave your training.

4. Thank everyone for attending. Consider giving participants certificates for their participation in the workshop, or check into whether participants can receive credit toward staff development/professional learning units.

Additional Resources

Recommended Readings

Goodstein, Anastasia. 2007. *Totally wired: What teens and tweens are really doing online.* New York: St. Martin's Griffin.

Kowalski, Robin M., Susan P. Limber, and Patricia W. Agatston. 2008. *Cyber bullying: Bullying in the digital age.* Malden, MA: Blackwell Publishing.

Magid, Larry, and Anne Collier. 2006. *MySpace unraveled: A parent's guide to teen social networking.* Berkeley, CA: Peachpit Press.

Willard, Nancy E. 2007. *Cyberbullying and cyber threats: Responding to the challenge of online aggression, threats, and distress.* New York: Research Press.

Willard, Nancy E. 2007. *Cyber-safe kids, cyber-savvy teens: Helping young people learn to use the Internet safely and responsibly.* New York: Jossey-Bass.

Online Resources

www.hazelden.org/cyberbullying This Web site is specific to this curriculum and also contains information about cyber bullying.

www.cyberbullyhelp.com This Web site includes general information about cyber bullying and information specifically targeted to parents, guardians, and students. Viewers of the site can also read excerpts from the book *Cyber Bullying: Bullying in the Digital Age.*

www.stopbullyingnow.hrsa.gov This interactive Web site sponsored by the U.S. Department of Health and Human Services provides extensive information about bullying with specific information about cyber bullying.

www.cyberbully.org The Center for Safe and Responsible Internet Use (CSRIU) provides an overview of cyber bullying along with downloadable documents of use to parents, guardians, and educators.

www.cyberbullying.org Along with its companion Canadian site www.cyberbullying.ca, this is one of the original Web sites created to inform individuals about cyber bullying, how to protect oneself against being cyber bullied, and what to do if you are cyber bullied.

www.connectsafely.com An Internet safety site designed for parents, guardians, teens, and experts providing information designed to facilitate "smart socializing" online and through mobile phones. The site has great tips and information regarding the newest forms of technology.

www.isafe.org The i-SAFE organization was founded in 1998 to promote safe use of the Internet. From this international leader in Internet safety education, the i-SAFE site provides information for children, parents, guardians, educators, and law-enforcement officials.

www.wiredsafety.org An interactive Web site created by Internet privacy and security lawyer Parry Aftab, this site provides information about cyber bullying and related online abuses.

www.netsmartz.org Sponsored by the National Center for Missing and Exploited Children, NetSmartz.org is devoted to providing information about Internet safety to children, parents, guardians, educators, and law-enforcement officials.

www.webwisekids.org An interactive Web site for children, parents, guardians, educators, and law-enforcement officials, Web Wise Kids offers interactive programs based on real-world cases to help educate youth about online safety. Online resources and related links are also provided.

www.ikeepsafe.org Governors and their spouses and various law-enforcement agencies founded the Internet Keep Safe Coalition. Its Web site provides information about Internet safety to youth, parents, guardians, and educators.

www.cdc.gov/ncipc/dvp/electronic_aggression.htm This site, maintained by the Centers for Disease Control and Prevention, provides an overview of cyber bullying, as well as links to several articles published by leading researchers in the field of cyber bullying in a special issue of the *Journal of Adolescent Health.*

www.ed.gov/about/offices/list/os/technology/safety.html This Web site from the U.S. Department of Education offers a listing of Web sites devoted to Internet safety.

www.ncpc.org/topics/by-audience/parents/internet-safety Sponsored by the National Crime Prevention Council, this site provides Internet-safety information tailored to all groups, including youth, parents, guardians, educators, and law-enforcement officials.

www.fbi.gov/publications/pguide/pguidee.htm This Web site provides a downloadable guide for parents and guardians about keeping their children safe from the dangers posed by the Internet. A search of this Web site will show related publications for kids as well.

Video and Digital Resources

Cyberbullying: Cruel Intentions This ABC-sponsored news program focuses on cyber bullying. The program includes a discussion and role-play based on research conducted at Brigham Young University. The program can be ordered online at www.impactpublications.com.

Cyberbullies This program is oriented toward education and prevention. It includes a question-and-answer discussion of cyber bullying and is part of the Taking a Stand: The Bullying Prevention series. The program can be ordered through the Web site www.impactpublications.com.

Adina's Deck This 30-minute film is designed to disseminate information about cyber bullying to nine- to fifteen-year-olds. It has a companion Web site, www.adinasdeck.com, and a teacher's guide.

Ryan's Story and ***What You May Not Know*** When he was thirteen, Ryan Patrick Halligan died by suicide as a result of being cyber bullied. His parents have now created a Web site, www.ryanpatrickhalligan.org, and two DVDs focusing on Internet safety, bullying, specifically cyber bullying, and suicide. Ryan's story includes a companion teacher's guide that allows teachers to discuss why bullying occurs, the effects on the person who is bullied, the role of bystanders, and how to deal with bullying when it does occur. Find more information about these DVDs on Ryan's Web site.

References

Arseneault, Louise, Elizabeth Walsh, Kali Trzesniewski, Rhiannon Newcombe, Ashalom Caspi, and Terrie E. Moffitt. 2006. Bullying victimization uniquely contributes to adjustment problems in young children: A nationally representative cohort study. *Pediatrics* 118:130–38.

Eisenberg, Marla E., Dianne Neumark-Sztainer, and Cheryl Perry. 2003. Peer harassment, school connectedness, and academic achievement. *Journal of School Health* 73:311–16.

Fekkes, Minne, Frans I. M. Pijpers, and S. Pauline Verloove-VanHorick. 2004. Bullying behavior and associations with psychosomatic complaints and depression in victims. *Journal of Pediatrics* 144:17–22.

Juvonen, Jaana, Sandra Graham, and Mark A. Schuster. 2003. Bullying among younger adolescents: The strong, the weak, and the troubled. *Pediatrics* 112:1231–7.

Kowalski, Robin M., and Susan P. Limber. 2007. Electronic bullying among middle school students. *Journal of Adolescent Health* 41:S22–S30.

Kowalski, Robin M., Susan P. Limber, and Patricia W. Agatston. 2008. *Cyber bullying: Bullying in the digital age.* Malden, MA: Blackwell Publishing.

Kowalski, Robin M., Susan P. Limber, Kimball Zane, and Tyler Hassenfeldt. 2008. Cyber bullying: Bullying in the digital age. Paper presented at the annual meeting of the Southeastern Psychological Association, Charlotte, NC.

Lenhart, Amanda. 2007. Cyberbullying and online teens. Retrieved November 15, 2007 from http://www.pewinternet.org.

Olweus, Dan. 1993. *Bullying at school: What we know and what we can do.* New York: Blackwell Publishing.

Olweus, Dan, Susan P. Limber, Vicki Crocker Flerx, Nancy Mullin, Jane Riese, and Marlene Snyder. 2007. *Olweus bullying prevention program: Teacher guide.* Center City, MN: Hazelden Publishing.

Rigby, Ken. 1997. *Bullying in schools: And what to do about it.* Briston, PA: Jessica Kingsley Publishers.

Rigby, Ken, and Phillip T. Slee. 1993. Dimensions of interpersonal relations among Australian school children and their implications for psychological well-being. *Journal of Social Psychology* 133:33–42.

Willard, Nancy E. 2007. Educator's guide to cyberbullying and cyberthreats. Center for Safe and Responsible Internet Use. Retrieved November 15, 2007 from http://www.cyberbully.org.

About the Authors

Susan P. Limber, Ph.D.

Dr. Susan P. Limber is director of the Center on Youth Participation and Human Rights and professor of psychology at Clemson University. She is a developmental psychologist who received her master's and doctoral degrees in psychology at the University of Nebraska–Lincoln. She also holds a master's of legal studies from Nebraska.

Dr. Limber's research and writing have focused on legal and psychological issues related to youth violence, particularly bullying among children, child protection, and children's rights. She directed the first wide-scale implementation and evaluation of the *Olweus Bullying Prevention Program* in the United States and coauthored the *Blueprint for the Bullying Prevention Program,* as well as many other articles on the topic of bullying. In recent years, she has directed the training for the *Olweus Bullying Prevention Program* in the United States. She has provided consultation to the National Bullying Prevention Campaign, supported by the Health Resources and Services Administration.

In 1997, she received the Saleem Shah Award for early career excellence in psychology–law policy, awarded by the American Psychology–Law Society of the American Psychological Association (Division 41) and the American Academy of Forensic Psychiatry. In 2004, Dr. Limber received the American Psychological Association's Early Career Award for Psychology in the Public Interest.

Robin M. Kowalski, Ph.D.

Dr. Robin M. Kowalski is a professor of psychology at Clemson University. She obtained her doctoral degree in social psychology from the University of North Carolina at Greensboro. Her research interests focus primarily on aversive interpersonal behaviors, most notably complaining, teasing, and bullying, with a particular focus on cyber bullying. She is the author or coauthor of several books, including *Complaining, Teasing, and Other Annoying Behaviors; Social Anxiety; Aversive Interpersonal Behaviors; Behaving Badly; The Social Psychology of Emotional and Behavioral Problems;* and *Cyber Bullying: Bullying in the Digital Age.* Her research on complaining brought her international attention, including an appearance on NBC's *The Today Show.*

Dr. Kowalski has received several awards, including Clemson University's Award of Distinction, Clemson University's College of Business and Behavioral Science Award for Excellence in Undergraduate Teaching, the Phil Prince Award for Excellence and Innovation in Teaching, and the Clemson Board of Trustees Award for Faculty Excellence.

Patricia W. Agatston, Ph.D.

Dr. Patricia W. Agatston is coauthor of the book *Cyber Bullying: Bullying in the Digital Age* with Robin M. Kowalski, Ph.D., and Susan P. Limber, Ph.D., recently published by Blackwell Publishing. She is also a nationally certified trainer and technical assistance consultant for the *Olweus Bullying Prevention Program.* She has been quoted in articles on cyber bullying in *Time Magazine* and *Good Housekeeping* magazine and has appeared on *Mom Talk Radio* and *Mornings* with Lorri Allen and Larry Estepa on FamilyNet Television. She was a participant in the CDC's expert panel on Electronic Media and Youth Violence and has presented nationally and internationally on cyber bullying.

Dr. Agatston is a licensed professional counselor (LPC) with the Cobb County School District's Prevention/Intervention Center in Marietta, Georgia. A founding board member for SafePath Children's Advocacy Center in Marietta, Georgia, Dr. Agatston received the Coalition for Child Abuse Prevention's VIP Award in 2005.